QUICKFLIP AUTO

HOW TO BUY AND SELL CARS IN ORDER TO BRING EXTRA INCOME INTO YOUR HOUSEHOLD

Andrew D. Ferraro

Cover Design by James, GoOnWrite.com
Formatting by Polgarus Studio

Printed in the United States of America

To my lovely wife, Elizabeth, who took the writing of this book from dream to reality; thank you.

CONTENTS

CHAPTER ONE *Introduction* 1

CHAPTER TWO *Getting Started* 9

CHAPTER THREE *Getting to Know Your Market* 17

CHAPTER FOUR *Finding the Right Vehicles* 27

CHAPTER FIVE *Investment Assessment* 35

CHAPTER SIX *Sealing the Deal* 69

CHAPTER SEVEN *Now What?* 79

CHAPTER EIGHT *Automobile Rehabilitation* 83

CHAPTER NINE *The Resale Process* 89

CHAPTER TEN *Life Lessons and Experiences* 103

CHAPTER ELEVEN *Wrapping Up* 129

Contact Me! 131

CHAPTER ONE
Introduction

Who

My name is Andrew. I grew up busting and fixing my own vehicles on the back roads of South Carolina, and now I've created a lifestyle in which I can do what I love and make money doing it. The beautiful part of my business plan is that anyone can do it. There is no need to be a master mechanic, or a master painter, or a master anything really. I am by no means an expert in any part of the automobile industry, but I've still managed to be successful at what I do. If you like the idea of turning wrenches in order to bring extra income into your household, than QuickFlip Auto is for you.

I have discovered that there are a few foundational keys to success, which I will gladly share with you. The first is an appreciation for automobiles. It is possible to be successful at work which you do not enjoy… But I have found that success is much more attainable and valuable to those who do enjoy their work. Enjoyment and appreciation will keep you going, even on those difficult days when the solution to a problem seems to keep just out of reach.

The second key to success is perseverance. QuickFlip Auto is a really fun business plan, but it doesn't come without hard work. No matter what happens, don't let a vehicle get the better of you! Every problem has a solution, and you will often discover more than one solution for any given problem. I have had many frustrating days of my own, and occasionally a night's rest and a fresh mindset is all I need to tackle a difficult task. So don't ever give up; keep a clear mind and a positive, can-do attitude.

The third key to success is integrity. No matter how large or small you choose to grow your business, you will develop a reputation. It is completely up to you whether your reputation is good or bad; however, it has been my experience that those business people with integrity and a positive reputation are more inclined to develop a successful and healthy business.

As I stated earlier, anyone can follow this program and succeed at making money. If you have an appreciation for automobiles, the drive to persevere, and a moral compass that points towards integrity, my QuickFlip Auto program may be just the thing for you.

What

So what is the QuickFlip Auto business plan exactly? The term "flip" refers to the cycle in which an older or broken car is bought, fixed up or upgraded, and then resold for a profit. Not only does this process recycle a vehicle that might otherwise become just junk, but it gives your customer, who is in need of transportation, a reliable set of wheels, and it is also financially rewarding for you, the one who takes the time to rehabilitate and sell the vehicle in the first place.

Starting your own QuickFlip Auto business can be as cost effective as you want to make it. Of course, it would be easy to drop several grand on an old, classic fixer-upper, but that's not really what QuickFlip Auto is about.

I personally made my first purchase for less than one thousand dollars, and with a little time and elbow grease, I was able to double my investment when it came time to sell the car. I will get more into the details of this process later on in the book, but I mention it now to show you how profitable such a side business can be.

By using this method, you can pocket the profit and reuse your initial startup capital to purchase another vehicle, or you can roll over both the start-up capital and the profit into the purchase of a more expensive project.

QuickFlip Auto is not a get rich quick program. In addition to the foundational keys to success that we discussed above (appreciation for automobiles, perseverance, and integrity), making money by flipping cars requires hard work and patience, and it also means getting a little dirty every now and then.

With all that said, I have found my own side business to be a great source of fun and additional income. It has also allowed me the opportunity to teach my wife about vehicles, and has brought us closer together as we work through our various projects. There are many benefits to a side business such as QuickFlip Auto. It is simple, it is effective, and I am more than happy to share the secrets of the trade with you here in this book.

When

One of the best parts about this program is that you can do it completely in whatever spare time you have throughout your busy days and weeks. I work a full time job and my wife goes to school full time. Even with both of our busy daytime schedules, we've still managed a very successful side business with QuickFlip Auto.

The good news is that there will always be a demand for transportation. There is no pressure to rush your work and sell the car NOW, because there will always be new people in need of reliable vehicles. So take a breath and relax. Work when you can, and work when you want. Hopefully your QuickFlip Auto business will become a source of enjoyment and relaxation in itself.

Where

I work out of my garage for most repairs, but I also try to be courteous to my neighbors; if a job looks like it is going to take a lot of time and space and look messy, I usually move my operation to the backyard.

Generally, neighbors won't care if you work on your automobiles in the garage or the driveway, but no one likes to see a mess across the street *every* time they look out their front window. Just remember to tidy up as you go, and no one will care if you replace a starter or change the oil in the driveway.

Occasionally, I send some vehicles out for repairs if the job is above my skill level. Every once in a while I happen across a car that has an issue that only the brand specific dealership can fix. I try to avoid purchasing vehicles with this sort of caveat because dealerships can, and will, charge more for their services; in fact, in my experience dealerships tend to charge almost double what auto repair shops charge.

Other jobs that I have sent out for have included a Corvette which needed a total paint job, and a Bronco with an electrical issue that was beyond the capabilities of my tools and equipment. As you begin working, you will work out your own system of which problems you can handle yourself and which problems are best sent to a more highly skilled expert. We'll touch on outsourcing jobs in more detail later on as we get deeper into the rehabilitation process.

The main point here is that QuickFlip Auto can be operated just about anywhere you have space. Have a driveway? Great. Have a garage? Perfect. Have a backyard? Fantastic. Any space you can fit a car will be enough space to fix the typical issues you will face in fixer-upper vehicles.

Why

I started this side business because I wanted to provide a nice living for my family. There is nothing worse than feeling the daily strain of debt and the nagging worry of how the bills are going to get paid. Living under these stresses is not healthy for the individual, and it's certainly not healthy for relationships. Believe me, I know!

QuickFlip Auto hasn't led me to "get rich quick," but it has allowed me to throw off the day to day stress of debt and bills; and let me tell you, financial freedom is a fantastic feeling! Not only have we been able to pay off our debts with QuickFlip Auto, but we have also been able to spoil ourselves with little vacations here and there, which is always refreshing!

My long term goal is to build this income stream until I have the financial flexibility to open a used car dealership, or to use my funds to springboard myself into another line of business. I have been working on this business for a couple of years now and have been successful enough to believe that, should I choose to do so, I will be able to open a small dealership within the next year.

Whether or not this is the route you want to go is completely up to you. Some people may want to keep their side business as simple as possible and work project to project; this is perfectly acceptable. QuickFlip Auto is a flexible business plan that allows each person to work at his or her own pace for his or her own goals. Whether you want to eventually open a dealership, become debt free, or just have some extra vacation money, QuickFlip Auto can certainly help you fulfill your needs.

How

The first few pages of this book serve to introduce you to the world of QuickFlip Auto. If you think you have what it takes to bring extra income into your home, I invite you to keep reading. The rest of the contents of this book will guide you along the nitty gritty details of the QuickFlip Auto program, and then it's all up to you. Your success is as great or as modest as you wish to make it! Good luck![1]

---

[1] Wrench Tip: Keep an eye out for Wrench Tips, found throughout the book at the bottom of the pages. If you are reading this book digitally, the Wrench Tips will be found at the back of the text. I use Wrench Tips to share the valuable bits of knowledge and advice that have served me well over the years. I hope that they will be as beneficial to you as they have been to me!

CHAPTER TWO
Getting Started

So you have decided that you are ready to get the ball rolling on your own QuickFlip Auto business, and you're chomping at the bit to get started. I am here to assure you that yes, you too can really have your own QuickFlip Auto business, and it is inexpensive and simple to begin!

This is what you will need to get started:

- A basic understanding of how to make simple repairs to vehicles
- A place to work
- $300.00-$1,000.00 dollars for start-up capital
- Basic negotiating skills
- The ability to fight procrastination and begin working right now![2]

---

[2] Wrench Tip: Personal motivation and the ability to fight procrastination will be the driving force behind your income. This is the case with any sales oriented business, whether you are selling something as cheap as ice cream, as expensive as luxury homes, or as awesome as vehicles.

You will also want to have a basic set of tools. Beyond making sure you have the essentials, you'll want to minimize up-front costs by holding off on purchasing any sort of specialty tools or materials until either your profits can pay for whatever it is, or you absolutely need it to fix a problem and get a car sale-ready.

Here are some of the tools that you are likely to find useful for your typical fixer-upper projects:

- Socket Set (This is one tool set that you will definitely find it worthwhile to spend the extra cash for quality! I can't even count the number of cheap socket wrenches that I have broken in the past.)[3]
- Breaker Bar (This is just a pipe that fits over the handle of a socket wrench. It can be used when you need a little more leverage to get the job done.)
- Screw Drivers (Flat head and Phillips)
- Pliers (Standard and needle nose)

---

[3] Wrench Tip: The primary issues with a cheap socket wrench is that when it breaks it usually means that you've busted your knuckles and the job is on hold until you get a new socket wrench. This can be very frustrating and can really derail what would have otherwise been a successful day. In my younger days I was more willing to risk the busted knuckles to save a few bucks; but with age comes wisdom, and I am now more than happy to spend the extra money if it means saving me both my time and my knuckles! I suggest looking into Craftsman or Cobalt for a quality socket set.

- Vise-Grip Pliers (Also known as "locking pliers," vise-grip pliers are a very handy do-it-all sort of tool.)
- Wire Cutters
- Jumper Cables
- Car Battery Charger[4]
- Floor Jack and Jack Stands[5]

As for hardware, I recommend not stocking up on various rigs and doodads before you know exactly what pieces and parts a project calls for. No matter how much hardware you buy ahead of time, you will likely never have all of the exact nuts and bolts you need. When the need does arise for a specific bolt, simply buy a few extra at that time. Chances are that if you need a bolt for one project, you will need that same bolt on another project in the future. Here are a few common items that you will find yourself needing now and again:

- Screws
- Bolts
- Electrical Wire

---

[4] Wrench Tip: Owning your own portable car battery charger is convenient; however, most auto parts stores will charge your car battery for free if you can spare the couple of hours of wait-time.
[5] Wrench Tip: When it comes time to do work under your vehicle, spare no expense for safety. Use a decent quality floor jack and at least two strong and sturdy jack stands; the more the merrier when it comes to jack stands!

- Fuses
- Heat Shrink Tubing (This helps seal up a wire fuse when a flame is held to the tubing.)

Fluids on the other hand are a different story. I recommend that you look closely at this list and consider stocking up on a few of these items before you begin your first project. One of the most important things that you can do to keep your automobiles in proper working order is to monitor their fluids. Having the proper fluids on hand can be the difference between a project taking three hours or three days. I have listed below a few fluids that I suggest keeping on hand in your garage, or even with you in your vehicle, for those just in case situations.

- Three Quarts of Oil (This will be enough so that you don't have to stop working to make an oil-run in the middle of a job. It's also a good idea to keep a quart of oil with you when driving a recently purchased vehicle, at least until you know for certain that the automobile is functioning reliably.)[6]
- Three Quarts of Transmission Fluid (Again, this will be enough so that you don't have to stop

---

[6] Wrench Tip: A typical vehicle will require five quarts of oil at all times in order to function properly. However, if you are in a pinch, you can run a motor on just three quarts of oil until you either reach an auto parts store or finish an ongoing project.

working to make a trip to the auto parts store. I recommend keeping a quart of transmission fluid in a new project vehicle until you know with certainty that the automobile is functioning reliably.)

- One Pint of Brake Fluid
- One Pint of Power Steering Fluid
- One Quart of Gear Oil
- Five Gallons of Gas
- One Gallon of Antifreeze
- Acetone or Paint Thinner
- WD40
- Liquid Wrench (Spray this on rusty old bolts before you start wrenching on them in order to help loosen them up.)
- Carburetor Cleaner
- Starter Fluid

There are also a few items that aren't so much related to getting your vehicles running as to keeping you, the mechanic, happy and comfortable. It is important to stay cool, calm, and collected. You will make your money off of problems that others couldn't – or wouldn't – solve themselves. Keep a clear mind, and stay comfortable. Have towels around to clean up messes and wipe your hands on, and use a light to look into a motor compartment instead of squinting through the shadows or feeling around blindly.

This advice may seem like common sense as you read it, but it's very easy to get caught up in the heat of the moment while you're working on a project. Short term convenience (not wasting time by walking around the car to grab the flashlight, or pausing to drink some water, or laying out a towel for padding before you spend the next hour working on your back) will never be able to justify the long term cost that you might risk inflicting on your health (headaches and tired eyes from squinting in the dark, dehydration, an injured back, etc.).

- Shop Towels (You don't necessarily have to buy these if you have plenty of old towels or t-shirts that could be used instead.)
- Flashlights (I recommend having two or three flashlights with fresh batteries, including a magnetic one. Magnetic flashlights allow you to keep both hands free while you work.)
- Fan or A/C unit (Garages can get pretty hot during summer time!)
- *Water (It is very important to stay hydrated properly, especially when you are hard at work. I recommend that you drink lots of water and stay away from any alcoholic drinks until the day's work is done.)[7]

---

[7] Wrench Tip: As refreshing as a cold one can be sometimes, beer and motors do not mix. Getting the job done efficiently and correctly requires steady hands and a sharp mind. So I

And of course, there will be messes. I know that cleaning up is probably not many peoples' favorite part of the day; but it is important to keep your project, your workspace, and yourself as presentable as possible, especially on a show day. There are a few very important cleaning items that will make this process a lot easier and less frustrating for you:

- Kitty Litter (If you accidentally spill any oil on the driveway, kitty litter will soak it out of concrete with no problem.)
- Bleach
- Tire Cleaner
- Tire Shine (Make sure that your tire shine is dry before you go for a ride. Wet tire shine will spin off onto your paint and make your car look dirty. Tire shine is an oil-based substance so it is difficult to clean off paint once it gets there.)
- Engine Degreaser
- Car Wash Solution
- Carpet Cleaner
- Glass Cleaner (If the vehicle you are working on has tinted windows, be sure that you use a glass cleaner that is safe for window tint. Ammonia is

---

recommend that you focus on the work first, and relax with a cold one only after you're done for the day.

found in many household glass cleaners and will turn window tint purple.)[8]

- Wax (I've always preferred the spray on wax because it is quick, it works, and it smells fresh.)
- Armor All
- Orange Hand Cleaner with Pumice (Nothing beats this stuff when it comes to getting greasy stains off your hands!)

Don't be put-out by the wish lists above. You certainly do not NEED all of these things, especially as you are just getting started; they are just items that I have found handy to have around as I have progressed through my various automobile projects.

As with any endeavor, it is important to avoid over-investing in infrastructure. It is easy to get excited over a new business idea or a new project. But you could easily go broke if you start by purchasing all of the latest and greatest automobile mechanic tools and toys, so go with the bare necessities and fill up your tool shed or garage only as quickly as your business success and your wallet allow!

---

[8] Wrench Tip: I have made a habit of not keeping any ammonia based cleaners in the garage. This helps me eliminate any possibility of grabbing the wrong cleaner and accidentally ruining a vehicle's window tint.

CHAPTER THREE
Getting to Know Your Market

Before you go rushing out to buy your first vehicle, it is important that you do some market research first. You need to monitor your market in order to determine if your community is capable of supporting a trade in used cars, and you also need to know what sellers have to offer and what buyers are looking for. Most communities have more than enough need for used vehicles to support your business; but if you live in a particularly sparsely populated area, you may find that you have to advertise to the market of the nearest town or city rather than to your local market.

The concept of supply and demand is important to keep in mind when beginning any new business endeavor, and QuickFlip Auto is no different.

Supply in this case is represented by the size of the existing used car market in your area. You need a decent amount of supply in your market, because you want to have plenty of availability of new inventory to choose from. Yet, too much supply means that customers will have more options for themselves, and this will drive down used car sales prices.

Demand is represented by how quickly these used cars are being bought. And of course, the more demand, the better, so you will want to monitor how quickly or slowly used cars are being sold and act accordingly.

A proper balance of supply and demand means that you are in an area with a strong used car market. A strong used car market will be apparent if used cars spend only a short amount of time for sale. A weak market means that used cars stay on the market for weeks or even months before being sold. So, if that truck you drove past on the side of the road, or that sedan you saw online, disappears after only a day or two, chances are that you are in a strong used car market.[9]

In order to get a handle on the supply and demand for used cars in your market area, you will need to do a little bit of research. There are a couple of ways that you can do your market research. You can take the hands-on route and take a drive through your town or city and observe the types of vehicles you see people driving most often. Are most of the vehicles work trucks? Or are they smaller, gas

---

[9] Wrench Tip: Another sign of a strong market is the rate of turnover for online advertisements on websites such as Craigslist.com. I classify a good market as having a turnover of seventy-five to one hundred new used car advertisements per day. You will know these ads are new because you will be monitoring the market daily, and you will be able to clearly pick out the new ads from the reposted older ads.

efficient cars? Are they spacious family SUVs, or are they sporty convertibles? Knowing which type of vehicles your market centers upon and making your purchases based on the patterns that you discover will give you a serious edge when it comes time to start buying and selling.

Another way to do your market research is the more hands-off approach. This method consists mostly of internet research. Log on to websites that facilitate auto sales, such as autotrader.com or craigslist.com, a few times a week. What kinds of vehicles are people in your area most desperate to get rid of, and why? What kinds of vehicles are people trying to trade for or buy? Are people most concerned about having cold air conditioning or four-wheel drive? Better fuel economy or low mileage?

Watch to see how long certain advertisements stay online. The turnover rate in advertisements can tell you a lot about which used cars are selling the best. For instance, do the advertisements for two-door Jeeps stay up longer than the advertisements for extended cab Chevrolets, or is it vice versa? If Jeeps sell better than Chevys in your market, your best bet will be to follow the trend and invest in the Jeep rather than the Chevy. The answers to questions like these will guide you toward making smarter investments, and as a result, more money.

Market research is a great way to get to know what I like to call your "seller pool" and your "buyer pool." In many business models these pools consists of two different sets of people found in two separate venues. For instance, a major grocery store's seller pool will consist of large manufacturers and wholesale produce growers, while its buyer pool will consist of the local customers who come in to buy their groceries every day. The techniques used by the grocery store to contact and do business with its seller pool are much different from the techniques it uses to contact and do business with its buyer pool.

QuickFlip Auto is unique in that this seller-buyer differentiation is not necessarily the case. Both sellers and buyers can be found in the same source pool, and you can contact and conduct business with sellers just the same as you would do with buyers.

Let me show you what I mean. My source pool consists of the following sources:

- Craigslist.com
- Autotrader.com
- Govdeals.com
- Local Classified Advertisements
- Roadside Sales
- Networking with Friends and Neighbors

These sources provide me with the proper contacts I need to conduct both purchases and sales. Often, a person who is selling a used vehicle is doing so with the intention of buying a new one either immediately, or sometime in the future. One day you might find that someone you bought a vehicle from will want to work with you again, this time to make their own purchase.

I say this because the truth is that a car is a car is a car. Whether or not someone buys a 2010 Jeep Wrangler from you or from Dealer Joe, they are getting the same vehicle with maybe only minor differences in cosmetics and miles. It is the person selling the car that really makes all the difference in sealing the deal or having the customer walk away.

Human beings are creatures of habit and comfort. Full disclosure, honesty, and a great attitude will do more to bring in business than all the polish and shine in the world. If people feel at ease around you and trust you, they will use your business again in the future, and they will recommend you to family and friends. This is one of the reasons it is very important to conduct your business with integrity, as I spoke about in the introduction to this book. You never know when you'll meet someone again, or where a lead for a good sale or a reference for a prospective buyer will come from.

Staying intimately familiar with your market pool by monitoring your sources will keep you on top of market swings and give you access to the best deals available. You will be able to determine what sells best and at what price. You will be able to speak with confidence when dealing with buyers and sellers.

Connecting with buyers is actually very simple; in fact, most of the time the buyer will be reaching out to you. When a buyer responds to one of your advertisements, you will want to get back with him or her as soon as possible. If someone is perusing for a new vehicle, chances are that he or she will be contacting a few different people about a few different vehicles. Getting that person in your car first will give you a distinct advantage over your competition.

This doesn't mean that you should be too eager to sell though. If the customer isn't serious about the deal, or if he gives you a "low-ball" offer, politely show him the door. There is no use wasting your time on tire-kickers when there are plenty of other buyers who are willing to pay the right price for the right car.

Connecting with sellers is also simple, but it usually requires that you make the first contact. There are several different types of sellers that you will encounter throughout your business. I will start with the two types of sellers that I find particularly easy to work with. I categorize these folks by where they place their value. In the used car market, value usually boils down to either time or money.

The seller who values his time more than his money is the seller who just cringes at the thought of toying around with internet advertisements and dealing with finicky buyers. His time is precious, and he would much rather just sell the car and be done with it. In this situation, I often find that sellers are quite willing to accept a lower price if it means a quick and easy sale. Whereas this type of seller sees more value in selling for less as long as its sooner, I generally have the time and patience to do the work and wait the couple days or weeks it takes to sell the car for full price.

The seller who values his money over his time is the seller who will sit on a vehicle for weeks or even months, waiting for it to sell but not wanting to put in the money to make it worthwhile for buyers. In this case, I contact the seller and let him know that I flip vehicles, and that I am interested in refurbishing his car or truck. I will offer a lower price in order to compensate for the work that I intend on putting into the vehicle. Usually these sellers are willing to see the upside in this situation and make a deal. This type of seller sees more value in his money than in his time, and is reluctant to shell out the money to fix what could be a decent vehicle.

It is important to find out which type of seller you are dealing with so that you can approach your negotiations from a stronger leverage point. Is your seller the type that values his time over his money? Or is he the type that values his money over his time? Either way, I see myself as offering a valuable service to the seller. I am willing to fulfill the need that he cannot or will not fulfill himself in exchange for something he values more, such as time or money. As long as the seller understands the value in the services I have to offer, he or she will usually be more than willing to take me up on a lower, but still reasonable, offer.

Occasionally you might run into a seller that isn't quite so cooperative. There are three types of sellers that I have found difficult, or even impossible, to work with. The first is the seller that wants more than the actual value of the vehicle simply because it is his vehicle. Some owners tend to think more highly of their vehicles because they have become emotionally attached. In this case, you do not want to spend the extra money to cover the cost of sentimental value. The only value that should be driving your investment purchases is actual value, and sentimental sellers often have a hard time coming to terms with the difference between sentimental and actual value.

The second type of difficult seller is the seller who wants exactly what his vehicle is worth. There is no problem with this of course; in fact, kudos to the seller for knowing the accurate value of his vehicle and sticking to his guns. The only problem with purchasing from this sort of seller is that you have a business to run and a profit to make. You and I need to purchase vehicles below their actual market value in order to be able to flip it later for a profit. So my recommendation is that you let sellers who are determined to get the market value from their vehicle do just that. There are plenty of other sellers out there who are more than willing to negotiate a purchase price.

The third type of difficult seller is the seller who is offering a competitive price on a particular vehicle, and knows it, and so he refuses to budge off the asking price (This is the type of seller that I recommend you become when it is your turn to sell a vehicle!). Like the last seller, this person most likely knows exactly what his vehicle is worth, and knows that he is offering a good deal on the asking price. The issue arises when the good deal just isn't quite good enough. Knowing he is offering a lower-than-market-value price, this type of seller is close-minded to further negotiations. And although the deal may be good, sometimes good just doesn't leave you enough wiggle room to make a profit later. Make sure you don't accidentally talk yourself into accepting a deal like this. Always keep in mind the maximum price you can afford to spend while still being able to make a profit.

These three types of sellers can often be more hassle than they are worth. I recommend that you end contact with a seller as soon as you recognize that he might fall into one of these categories. A lot of time can be wasted on dead end deals like these, and I have found that my time is better spent searching for those more flexible sellers.

In addition to looking for vehicles that are being advertised for sale, I recommend advertising that you buy vehicles as well. This can be done through roadside signs, also known as "bandit signs," through classified advertisements in the local newspaper, or on websites such as Craigslist.com.[10] This will give those sellers who need cash immediately an opportunity to skip the advertising process completely, and be guaranteed a quick sale. It is also much easier and less offensive to negotiate a lower

---

[10] Wrench Tip: You will receive your best prices from sellers who approach you through "I Buy Used Cars" advertisements. Sellers who actively seek out buyers in this manner are typically in a situation in which they need to sell quickly, and at any price. Usually, sellers responding to these "I Buy Used Cars" ads will be selling their vehicles for very low prices. The motivation of sellers in this situation is to quickly find a buyer who is willing to pay more than the junk yard will pay.

purchasing price when the seller is approaching you, rather than you approaching the seller.

However, please keep in mind that I am not advocating shady deals or ripping off desperate people. If I can meet my necessary profit margins and still give the seller a fair price, he's got a deal. What I will never do is talk a distressed seller further down on the price simply because I can tell he's in a tight spot. I will only ever make a deal that is fair to both sides and gives the seller and buyer each what they need.

So, now you have some background information on supply and demand, market research, and how to reach out to buyers and sellers. Now it's your turn. Go ahead and drive around your town and surf the web. Information is power, and the more information you have before you start doing business, the more prepared you will be and the better deals you will be able to make. Feel free to use my source pool as a foundation for creating your own, and get to know your market so that you know what sells and what doesn't in your area. Good luck, and have fun with your research. Keep an eye out for good deals, and next chapter we will begin to go through the process of how to buy your first automobile.

CHAPTER FOUR
Finding the Right Vehicles

The Vehicle Profile System

When you are buying a vehicle with the intent to profit from its sale it is important to always keep in mind what you want out of the deal, and that is financial profit. I call this "beginning at the end." I buy vehicles so that I can sell them as soon as possible, at a price that leaves me with a nice profit. At the end of the day you want to buy the right car at the right price. This means that you will be sifting through a lot of potential deals in order to find the one that meets your needs. In order to pick out the best deals, you should have a profile in mind, a specific mold into which your ideal vehicles will fit.

When I first started to really make money with my QuickFlip Auto business, I began to lose a bit of my focus as well. I found myself driven a little more by fun, and a little less by profit. For instance, I once bought an 84 Chevy Corvette for $2,000.00. Fun it certainly was, but a good business investment it was not. I found out the hard way that utility vehicles like Chevy Blazers sell much better in my market area than sporty cars like Chevy

Corvettes. I did not consider at all how much I would be limiting myself when it came time to resell the car. My pool of buyers became much smaller because the car didn't fit the functional needs of the demographic in my location.

After spending $700.00 on a new paint job for the Corvette and a few bucks here and there for administrative fees such as registration and taxes, I had a little over $2,700.00 tied up in the car. I was only eventually able to sell it for $3,200.00, which left me with a profit of less than $500.00. It took me several months to sell the car; during which I had to grit my teeth and watch many good deals come and go, as most of my investment capital remained tied up in the Corvette.

I learned a valuable lesson from my experience with the Corvette, and I quickly put myself back on track. In order to prevent myself from straying from my business plan again in the future, I began to develop what I call my "vehicle profile system." This system is designed to keep me focused on making purchases with my market area demographic always in mind.

For instance, my target demographic is what I would classify as a "utility market." The folks that live in my city tend to prefer useful vehicles rather than showy vehicles, and 24/7 reliability tends to trump gas consumption when it comes to important vehicle attributes. Because I have taken the time to get to know these and other details about my market, I know that my vehicle profile calls for a practical car, truck, or SUV with reasonable miles (under

200,000 mandatory, under 150,000 preferred), presentable interior, decent tires, and in acceptable mechanical condition. The vehicle does not have to be cosmetically perfect on the exterior, but it should still be respectable in that there are no crushed-in doors or rust patches that have corroded straight through the body. A vehicle that fits this description is very likely to fit someone in my market area who is looking for a new used vehicle.

My vehicle profile system also takes into account my equipment, my capabilities, and my resource assets. There is no point in me purchasing a vehicle, even if it meets the needs of my utility-market to the letter, if it has an issue or some sort of damage that I can't fix or repair. For instance, I won't touch vehicles that have mysterious knocking sounds in the engine, or vehicles that spew black smoke. I acknowledge that these issues have the potential to be beyond my equipment or my capabilities, and so the vehicle does not fit within my vehicle profile. I thank the seller for his time and move on to a find a different deal for a vehicle that does fit my profile.

Resource assets are a valuable part of the QuickFlip auto business plan. Having great resources can be the extra edge you need in order to take on a project that you would otherwise be unable to tackle. For instance, a year or so ago I found a great auto electric shop just down the road that does top-grade work quickly and at a fair price. This resource has allowed me to expand my investments to include vehicles that may have electrical issues that I would otherwise be unable to fix on my own. Other good resources to have are those such as an inexpensive body shop and a reliable used tire dealer.

Once you do find a reliable and fairly priced resource, make sure to maintain any connections you make with the people who work there.[11] Continue to bring your vehicles to that same place and you will continue to receive great service, and possibly even discounted prices depending on how often you bring in business. The connections you make through your trusted resource assets will also be able to spread the word about your business and send potential customers your way. Networking is a great way to expand your business!

Just as it can be easy to lose sight of your market demographic, it can also be easy to lose sight of your personal limitations. An easy way to ensure that you don't exceed the limits of your equipment, capabilities, and resource assets on any investment project is to create a list of minimum standards that every vehicle you buy must fit into. While it's okay to mark things off of this list as you gain more equipment and experience, and as you broaden your network and create new beneficial relationships; just

---

[11] Wrench Tip: You wouldn't want to tick off the guy at the drive-through fast food window before you get your food, and the same goes for the people working on your cars. It is very important to be nice to the people who work on your vehicles. A little kindness can go a long way, so always smile and be friendly!

remember to keep your actual right-now capabilities in perspective.

Below is a list of the minimum standards that I follow. These standards have helped me protect myself from getting burnt on bad deals, and helped me also to prevent myself from making emotional decisions.

Here are a few of the minimum standards on my own list:

- The vehicle runs and drives. (If you have a car trailer and can accurately identify the issue preventing a vehicle from running, perhaps you can cross this off your list of minimum standards.)
- The vehicle has decent tires. (The cost of good tires adds up quickly, and while buyers will want to buy a vehicle that won't need the tires replaced immediately, I have found that brand new tires don't significantly raise the value of older vehicles. This being the case for my market area, I prefer to purchase vehicles that already have tires with at least fifty percent tread left.)[12]
- The interior should be presentable or repairable.
- There should be no permanent bad smells or odors.

---

[12] Wrench Tip: If you have a good used tire dealer around your area, you can usually pick up a decent set of used tires for around a hundred dollars. You just want to be careful when driving on used tires; because, after all, someone traded them in for a reason!

- The motor should run without any knocking or tapping sounds.
- The transmission should shift smoothly between gears.
- If there are any fluids leaking, I need to know from exactly where.
- The vehicle should not be titled as a salvaged or rebuilt vehicle. (I tend not to trust the tinkering of previous owners, but this decision is really up to your own discretion.)[13]
- The vehicle should not have any electrical ghosts. (By electrical ghost, I mean a situation such as the radio only working when the lights are on.)
- The vehicle must have a title.

As we've seen throughout this chapter, my vehicle profile system has (and yours should, too) four layers; my target market demographic; my ideal vehicle profile; a clear understanding of my equipment, capabilities, and resource assets; and my list of minimum standards for making an investment decision.

---

[13] Wrench Tip: When it comes to used vehicles, the closer to stock condition, the better. A smart buyer will always prefer the as-close-to-stock-as-possible used vehicle over the salvaged or "owner improved" used vehicle. In my experience, the reason for this is that people tend not to trust the mechanical work of strangers, and for good reason too! Never trust a previous owner's handiwork until you have satisfactorily checked it out yourself.

This vehicle profile system has helped me stay on track with my investment purchases and has also allowed me to make more money in the long run by helping me make only the most strategic and intelligent decisions. I am hoping that by sharing this information with you, I am helping you to avoid the mistakes I made early on in the start of my business. I encourage you to take some time now and work out your own vehicle profile system and list of minimum standards.

CHAPTER FIVE
Investment Assessment

Initial Assessment of a Potential Investment

At this point, I hope that you have had time to do some market research and draw up a working outline of your vehicle profile system. The next step is to find your first investment vehicle. Looking through all the advertisements for vehicles online can be daunting. How do you decide which deals are the best to follow up on, and which deals are the best to avoid? This section of the book should get you started down the right track when it comes to sifting through all the vehicle investment possibilities out there.

The first thing I look at when I am examining an advertisement is the seller's motivation for getting rid of a vehicle.[14] I like to see reasons that tell a story about a

---

[14] Wrench Tip: Each car has a story. It is important to get the seller to tell you this story, in order for you to better understand what kind of vehicle you will be dealing with. The story will tell you why the seller purchased the vehicle in the first place, what the vehicle was used for, why it is now being sold, and much more. Listen to figure out if the seller speaks with frustration

vehicle that is still in good running order, but is simply no longer needed or wanted by the owner. These vehicles will still have plenty of life left, but the owners will already feel like they have gotten their money's worth out of them. This type of sale doesn't last long, so it is important to recognize these great deals quickly.

Here are some reasons for selling that I have come to recognize as green-light signals when it comes to contacting a seller with an offer on a vehicle:

- The seller has owned the car for years and has simply decided that it is time to upgrade to something newer.
- The seller is moving and can't or doesn't want to take the vehicle with him.
- The seller is expecting a new baby and needs a bigger vehicle.
- The seller had bought the vehicle for a daughter or son, but now the child has grown up and moved out, and no one uses the car anymore.
- The seller wants the cash for one reason or another more than he needs the car.

---

about the vehicle, or if he speaks of it fondly. Keep watch for any discrepancies among your different sources of information, such as what the seller is telling you, what you read in the advertisement, or what you see in the sales pictures.

- The seller loves the truck but got a new job and needs something easier on gas for the longer commute.
- The seller is going through a divorce and wants/needs to liquefy his assets.

These are all reasons that tell me the owner of a decent vehicle is simply ready to move on to something else. What I don't like to see are reasons for selling that paint a picture of a vehicle that is being replaced because it can no longer be relied upon. These sellers usually won't come right out and say that this is the reason they are selling their vehicles, so you'll want to look and listen a very closely to work through any nonsense.

Here are some red flags that you should watch out for when reading through an advertisement:

- Inconsistencies about the vehicle's history (If a seller says he's owned a vehicle for years but he can't seem to remember how the bumper got cracked, or if he forgets to tell you that the passenger seat, the one he didn't take a picture of, is torn up, then don't buy the vehicle! If an owner won't tell you up front about simple things like cosmetic issues, imagine what he's not telling you about mechanical issues or service history.)
- References to the vehicle as "a great project car" or a "handyman's special"

- Ambiguous phrases like "just needs a little TLC" that neglect to tell you what exactly the true issues are with the vehicle
- Disclaimers like "drove just fine when I parked it a year ago" that decline to comment on the current condition of the vehicle
- Sellers that don't own the vehicle, but who are selling it for a "buddy" (Don't get involved in three way deals like this if at all possible! Communication is frustrating, information doesn't get passed along, and there is no way to tell if a deal is legitimate until you match up the seller's ID with the vehicle's title. These deals are way more hassle than they are worth, and usually turn out to be shady somehow, or the seller might just be incompetent to the point that he is not worth dealing with.)[15]

Keep an eye out for these and any other red flags you might see in an advertisement. You are an honest business person who treats your buyers and sellers with integrity,

---

[15] Wrench Tip: If there is a third party involved in a sale for the purpose of protecting a seller who cannot protect himself, such as a young person or an elderly person, working with the third party is not an automatic deal killer; but it is definitely a red flag that you will want to look into. Ask plenty of questions, and be quick to beat feet away from a deceptive third party, or a third party that is far too emotionally involved to negotiate.

and you want to deal with people who will give you the same courtesy.

You need to get an accurate account of the vehicle you are considering purchasing and a solid feel for how much time and money you will have to put into it to make it sellable. This will be hard to do when dealing with crooked sellers, so I recommend not even wasting your time by contacting those who you think may be trying to pull a quick one. Follow your instincts and watch out for red flags!

The second thing I look at is the presentation of the vehicle for sale. You can tell a lot about the vehicle and the seller just by assessing a photo in an advertisement. The first thing I look for is to see how well, if at all, the vehicle has been cleaned up for the sales pictures. Are there dirty clothes strewn about in the back seat? Are there empty soda bottles on the floor boards? Does it look like there is something sticky on the steering wheel? These are all telltale signs that the seller put no effort into cleaning up the vehicle prior to reaching out to buyers.

This tells me two things; 1) the owner isn't serious about selling his vehicle if he didn't even bother to give it a quick once over, and negotiations with a disinterested seller will often go nowhere fast, and 2) if the owner hasn't cared enough to keep his car clean and presentable throughout the time that he has owned it, chances are he showed the same amount of initiative, or even less, when it came to the care and maintenance of the parts of the car not directly in sight – such as the brakes and the engine.

Chances are that such an owner hasn't kept up with regular maintenance tasks, such as changing the oil, rotating the tires, checking the serpentine belts, monitoring the fluids, and fixing any other little wear and tear items.

Be very careful about buying cars that have been driven for thousands and thousands of miles with little to no regular maintenance; this type of vehicle tends to turn into a quicksand trap, exhausting quickly both your budget and your time. As a principle, it is always best to buy a vehicle that you can tell has been cared for by its previous owner.[16]

On the other hand, if it is obvious that the owner did go through the trouble of detailing his vehicle before the sales pictures were taken, or before he parked it on the side of the road, this shows that he is invested in selling and that there is a good chance he took equally good care of the vehicle when it was still his primary means of transportation.

The sales pictures will also provide valuable insight into the lifestyle of the seller. Look carefully over the house if it is visible in the picture. Is it well kept, or not kept at all? Does the house have any flags or signs hanging? These

---

[16] Wrench Tip: Keep in mind that an automobile is a series of small machines that are all connected and working together as a single larger machine. The failure of one small system usually has a negative effect over time on each of the other connected systems, so be wary about purchasing poorly maintained vehicles. Mechanical issues tend to be infectious, spreading throughout the vehicle over time if left unchecked.

could be sports flags, nation flags, signs warning off solicitors, election signs, etc. Also look for distinguishing marks on the vehicle; such as political bumper stickers, flashy rims, or giant mud tires.

All of these clues will tell you how to negotiate with the owner. The more you know about the owner, the better you will be able to connect with him, and the happier both of you will be about the reaching an agreement.

I also look for what's NOT shown in the pictures of a vehicle for sale. Is there a section of the car that is blatantly not displayed in any of the photographs? Is only one of the front seats shown in the photographs, or is the interior not even shown at all? Does the advertisement mention "minor scratches" but neglect to display the damage to prospective buyers?

What's not shown in the pictures could be a huge deal, or it could simply be poor sales photography. Definitely make a note about anything you have questions about or that seems suspect to you, so that later on when you call the seller, you can hear what he has to say and listen for his reactions to your questions. You can never be too careful, especially when your money and your time are on the line![17]

---

[17] Wrench Tip: As you build your business, you will discover that time is a very valuable commodity. If you are running a healthy business, there will definitely come a time when there are not enough hours in a day. So waste less time now to have more time later!

The next thing I look at is how the advertisement or the "for sale" sign is written. This can tell you a lot about the seller and the way he does business. As I discussed above, you should always watch out for red flags that warn you if a seller is hiding something. If a deal sounds too good to be true, it might just be too good to be true. Also keep an eye out for the acronym "obo," which means "or best offer." If a seller tags this phrase onto his asking price in an advertisement or on a for-sale sign, you can immediately assume that there is plenty of room for negotiation in the bottom price.

You can use the text of the advertisement to get a feel for the personality of the seller. Is the advertisement sloppy? Is every other word spelled incorrectly? Does the advertisement use profanity? Is the advertisement written in an aggressive tone?

You truly can tell a lot about the seller by how he addresses his potential buyers; and take it from me, dealing with difficult sellers is just that – difficult! If you get a bad vibe from how a seller conducts himself through his advertisement, chances are the situation won't improve with a face-to-face meeting. On the other hand, if the advertisement is well presented and organized, you can expect the seller and his vehicle to be the same.

Also make sure that you read carefully what the seller has to say about the vehicle, and don't take his word for it. Do your own research. Look up the make and model of the car and double check the facts. You may find that the seller really has no idea what he is talking about, but is trying to sound impressive and make his vehicle out to be more than it really is.

Use sources such as Kelly Bluebook (www.kbb.com), Edmunds (www.edmunds.com), and NADA Guides (www.nadaguides.com) to price check the actual value of the used car.[18] These sources will provide you with valuable information throughout the entirety of your QuickFlip Auto business experience, and I highly suggest that you refer back to them on a regular basis.

For instance, after researching a vehicle you may find that a seller is asking a price that is too high and you can use the actual values provided by these free resources to negotiate a lower price. Or you might discover through your research that the seller is asking a below market price, in which case you will want to jump on the sale as long as the car is truly in good working order.

If you are looking at a roadside sale, you will have to make a judgment call without the chance to look over an extensive owner's write-up on the vehicle. The good news is that you can still tell quite a bit from a "for sale" sign. For example, if a seller is not willing to put the asking price on his sign, chances are he is fishing for high offers and will be asking for more than the vehicle is worth. Go ahead and give the number a call, but don't expect a

---

[18] Wrench Tip: Get familiar with KBB, Edmunds, and NADA. Notice how the values differ from source to source and how accurate the guides are with predicting how well certain vehicles sell in your area and at what prices. Use whatever guide turns out to be the most accurate regarding your market area.

reasonable first price. If a seller is serious about selling a vehicle, he will write the asking price on the sign. This will help him filter his phone calls down to just those buyers who are equally serious, who have had the opportunity to consider the asking price, and who are willing to get together and do business.

Above all else, when you are evaluating a potential investment, it is important to always remember that your purpose with QuickFlip Auto is to make money. Do your research, and don't let yourself make any decisions based on emotions. Becoming attached to the idea of purchasing a certain vehicle before you know all the facts will make it harder to recognize when what looks like a great deal, really isn't all that it might appear to be. Try to stay objective when researching potential investments, and if you feel yourself getting too emotionally charged up, step away for the night. Separate yourself from the immediacy of the situation and take some time to clear your head; the advertisement will be there tomorrow.

The worst thing that you could do is to allow yourself to become emotionally attached to a vehicle before the sale is complete. Make sure that you have a good handle on what you are looking at, and that you are seeing the vehicle for exactly what it is. And most importantly, you must be willing to walk away from a vehicle if you don't get the terms of sale exactly how you want them.[19]

---

[19] Wrench Tip: It is always better to miss out on a few good deals than to get hosed on a single bad deal. If there is any

Remember that the goal here is to make money. Your selling price will be equal to your investment plus your profit, or your investment minus your loss; so be very aware of the investments you make, and be honest with yourself and thorough when calculating the costs needed to turn an investment into a profitable sale. The best thing you can do for yourself and for your business is to remain cool, calm, and collected.

Initial Contact: Phone Interview

At this point, you will want to have taken down notes for a few different vehicles that you have found either online or alongside the road. These notes should include the name of the seller, the contact number, the make and model of the vehicle, the condition of the vehicle, and any other questions or comments that you might have about the vehicle. You will want to have these notes in front of you before you make first contact with the seller. Having all of your information and all of your questions prepared ahead of time will help the conversation go much more smoothly, and will make you sound like a more serious buyer.

---

question in your mind if a car you are looking at is really worth the investment...JUST WALK AWAY! Especially when you are just starting out, a financial loss will hurt you way more than an opportunity loss. There will always be more opportunities, but the same cannot always be said for money in your wallet if you unknowingly make a poor decision.

The phone interview is a very important part of the vehicle purchasing process. This is probably the first time that you will have made contact with the seller, and now is when you will both be getting a sense of how the other does business. Making a good first impression is crucial. The more the other person likes you and trusts you, the more likely he will be to want to make a deal with you. So use this phone interview process to get to know the seller just as much as you get to know the vehicle he is selling.

Ask plenty of questions, but don't come off as aggressive or overbearing when you do so. You will be trying to figure out how motivated the seller is to move the vehicle, and what his expectations are from the sale. He will be doing the same with you by trying to figure out how motivated you are to make the purchase.

The seller will most likely prefer to make a cash deal. A cash transaction is quick, clean, and simple. I always go to look at a vehicle with cash in hand; but I never tell the seller that I will be bringing the money unless it is advantageous for me to do so, or unless he very specifically asks. Letting the seller ask helps me gauge his likely sales experience and also how badly he needs to sell the car and make some cash.

In order to make this first phone conversation go smoothly, I suggest you write a generalized script that you can use for each of your inquiries. Keep it natural, you won't need to read from the script word for word, but you'll be using it more as a baseline instead. This will ensure that you get all the information you need, and will also give you a roadmap through the conversation in case you freeze up.

Below I have written out several of the questions that I like to ask sellers. I suggest that you work some of these into your script:

- Why are you selling the vehicle? (Refer back to the section in this chapter titled "Initial Assessment of a Potential Investment" for green lights and red flags to watch out for.)
- How set are you on the price?
- What has the vehicle been used for? (You'll want to listen carefully to the seller's answer to this question for any signs that the vehicle has been subjected to rough usage and abuse prior to being done up for the sale.)
- What do you like most about the vehicle? (At this time, you will likely get the run down on any upgrades or bells and whistles that the vehicle possesses.)
- What do you like least about the vehicle? (This opens up a safe way for the seller to address any negative information that he may have left off of the advertisement.)
- Have you had any other offers on the vehicle?
- Does the vehicle need any minor or major repairs?
- What do you think it would cost to get the vehicle in tip-top shape?

- What do you think the vehicle would be worth in perfect shape? (Of course, you should already know the answer to this question before you even call up the seller by using resources such as KBB, Edmunds, and NADA. Asking the seller again will give you a better handle on how highly he thinks of his vehicle, and will also soften the seller up to the idea of a lower price based on condition of his own vehicle as compared to the idea of mint condition.)

- Have you considered trading in the vehicle? At what price?

- Do you own the vehicle free and clear?

- If you still owe anything on the vehicle, how much? And what are your payments?

- Are you current on your payments?

- If I am willing to buy your vehicle, how quickly would you be willing and able to close on the deal?

- What are you looking to get out of the vehicle?

- When do you have time to show me the vehicle?

Sometimes I am able to get all of my questions answered, and other times I am only able to get a few answered before I go and see the vehicle with my own eyes. It depends on how willing the seller is to humor an inquisitive buyer, and how willing I am to work with difficult seller. Be wary of sellers who seem reluctant to answer your questions, but also be considerate to the fact that people only have so much time in one day. Don't take up any more time than you have to, and people will appreciate your understanding of their busy schedules.

Of course, if the car is just down the road and I can't seem to keep the seller on the phone long enough to answer my questions, I may just head over and ask in person. The only scenario under which I insist on having all the answers up front, is if the car is more than an hour away. I will very rarely drive this far to look at a vehicle, but if I do, I want to make sure the vehicle is worth my time and gas before I make the road trip.[20]

In this situation, I would also request that the seller not show the vehicle to anyone else before I arrive. He or she should be accommodating to your request, understanding that because you are willing to make the road trip to view the car, you are due the courtesy of the vehicle still being for sale upon your arrival. If you do feel the need to drive long distance for an investment, definitely make sure to formalize this agreement.

At this point, let's take a break and give you a chance to write up a brief practice script. Remember to include some of the questions I have written out above, and

---

[20] Wrench Tip: After driving a long distance to look at a vehicle, you will be more likely to make a purchase simply because you have already invested the time and gas money in making the trip. I suggest sticking to purchasing locally, at least until you get to the point where you are selling so many vehicles that you need to start reaching farther out for greater inventory.

definitely throw in any questions of your own as well. The more time you spend familiarizing yourself with your script and the questions you would like to ask, the more confident you will feel when speaking with the seller and the smoother the conversation will go. Here is an example script that I have written up to get you started:

You: Hi there, is this Mr. Seller?

Seller: Yeah, who's this?

You: My name is Andrew, how are you doing today?

Seller: Oh I'm doing all right.

You: Good, good. Well I'm calling you today because I'm looking at the vehicle you have for sale here on Craigslist. Can you tell me a little bit about the vehicle?

Seller: Oh yeah, of course. It's a great little truck… (At this point, the seller will explain what an excellent vehicle he is selling.)

You: Well that sounds good. Why are you selling it?

Seller: Well it was my son's truck, and he's gone off to school on the other side of the country, so it's just sitting in my driveway now taking up space.

You: Have you owned it long?

Seller: Well, let's see… Maybe about three, no, four years now.

You: Does it have any mechanical issues that you know of?

Seller: I've driven it for the last couple of days and it's done just fine for me. I'd be comfortable telling you it's mechanically sound. It's got a ding here and there though, but the motor is solid.

You: That's good to hear. It says in your ad that you're asking for $1,500.00, is there any wiggle room there?

Seller: Well I don't know. I may be able to budge a little. What are you thinking?

You: Well, here's my story, I do a little bit of buying and selling. I'd really like to purchase your vehicle and put some elbow grease into getting it up to tiptop shape. As the vehicle sits today I could probably give you $1,000.00 cash for it and we could move forward immediately. How does that sound to you? (At this point, don't say anything else until the seller speaks first!)[21]

---

[21] Wrench Tip: Time for your best poker face! In sales, the first person to speak after you present your pitch loses the upper hand…Make sure that it isn't you!

Seller: Hm, well, I was really hoping for fifteen hundred…but I don't know, maybe we can work something out.

You: Okay, let's do that. When would be a good time to come by and meet?

Seller: I'm available for the next couple of hours if you want to come by now.

You: Where at?

Seller: My place works best for me. The address is 123 Sparkplug Ln.

You: That sounds perfect. I'll be there in about twenty minutes.

Of course, some sellers will be more flexible with accepting lower offers than others. I definitely like to make sure that the seller and I are in the same ballpark on price before I go to look at any vehicle. If a seller isn't willing to negotiate, there is really no reason for me to go and waste my time looking at the vehicle he is selling. Even if I really like a vehicle, I always remind myself that my end goal is to make a profit; and I won't make a profit if I can't get the vehicle for the right price!

Appointment for Inspection

At this point, you have found a potential vehicle investment and you have made contact with the owner. You should have a pretty good idea of the condition of the vehicle based off of the information in the advertisement and the information gained throughout your phone conversation with the seller. Preferably you have already discussed the price with the seller as a precondition to making the trip to see the vehicle.

I always organize the cash I plan on taking with me beforehand, and I highly suggest that you do the same. I have picked up a couple of pointers about handling money before and during deals that I would like to pass on to you before you head off to make your first purchase.

First off, the larger the roll of cash, the more enticing the seller will find the deal. $1,000.00 in twenties will always look better than $1,000.00 in hundreds. The longer it takes to count the money, the better your seller will feel about selling his vehicle.

Secondly, you should never carry all of your cash in the same place. Separate your money into smaller portions and carry it in two different pockets.[22] One pocket should hold

---

[22] Wrench Tip: Another pointer here is to stack your money. I will use the example above to demonstrate what I mean. I am going to look at a vehicle with $1,000.00 in one pocket and $300.00 in the other. $1000.00 is my ideal purchase price, so that's fine, I just fold these bills in half and stick them in my pocket. The extra $300.00 is what I will spend if I have to in

the money that you would like to spend on a vehicle, and the other pocket should hold the additional amount that you are willing to throw in to sweeten the deal.

For instance, if I am willing to spend $1,300.00 on a vehicle, but would prefer to spend only $1,000.00, I will have the $1,000.00 in one pocket and the additional $300.00 in a different pocket. This allows me to make my initial offer of $1,000.00 without the seller seeing that I might have been willing to spend more.

Again though, be careful with how much you are willing to spend on top of your initial offer. Don't make an emotional decision and let yourself spend more on the purchase of a vehicle than you can get out of its sale. In order to keep between the lines, I've written myself a pricing guide, which I have included below. These numbers have worked well for me. I recommend using this chart as a guideline for your own QuickFlip Auto business.

---

order to make a deal. I will have this $300.00 pre-counted and arranged into three separate $100.00 stacks of neatly folded bills. I stick these in my other pocket, with the folded sides closest to the top of my pocket. This allows me to reach into my pocket in front of the seller and pull out one, two, or three stacks of additional bills, without giving away the information that I actually have more money in my pocket than I am pulling out. This allows me to raise the price to $1,100.00, $1,200.00, or $1,300.00, depending on how my negotiations are going.

The Vehicle Price Guide

VEHICLE PRICE GUIDE									
MARKET VALUE 1000	2000	3000	4000	5000	6000	7000	8000	9000	10000
MONEY INVESTED 500	1000	1500	2600	3250	3900	4550	5200	6300	7000
*This amount will include both the purchase price and cost of repairs									
SALE PRICE 900	1800	2700	3600	4500	5400	6300	7200	8100	9000
PROFIT EARNED 400	800	1200	1000	1250	1500	1750	2000	1800	2000

The first line of this chart represents the market value potential of the vehicle I am thinking about purchasing. Ideally, after you are done refurbishing the vehicle and fixing whatever issues it may have, it will be worth this value. I always make this assessment by using resources such as KBB, Edmunds, and NADA Guides.

The second line of the Vehicle Price Guide represents how much total money I should have invested into each project. For example, if I purchased a vehicle which had a potential market value of $3,000.00, I can look down my chart to see that if I want to make my normal profit, I must have no more than $1,500.00 total invested in the vehicle. This includes the sales price and any repairs, so keep this in mind when you are looking for a vehicle to purchase!

The third line of the Vehicle Price Guide is my ideal resale price. I like to keep my prices competitive so I will often sell a vehicle for slightly less than its market value. Take the vehicle above for example; I know that the car is worth $3,000.00 at its market value, and so I will price it at about $2,700.00 give or take, depending on the situation. This helps my vehicles sell quickly and also keeps my business rolling forward.

The fourth line of the Vehicle Price Guide is my estimated profit. If I can purchase a vehicle with the potential to be worth $3,000.00, invest only $1,500.00 in the purchase and repairs, and sell it for just below market value at $2,700.00, I know that I can make $1,200.00 profit.

Now, keep in mind, that these are the numbers that I have found to work for my business. If you find that these numbers are overly ambitious, or not ambitious enough, tweak them up or down however you feel is necessary. After all, it is your business that you will be running!

I do recommend that you use my Vehicle Price Guide at least as a template to create your own price guide. Having a standard pricing strategy and profit projection model will help you make good decisions and is essential to running a business successfully.

Physical Inspection

One thing that I like to remind myself when I am on my way to look at a new vehicle is that the price I am willing to pay is negotiable one way: downward. If I get to a vehicle and see that it is not up to snuff from what I had been led to understand by the advertisement and by the seller, I will drop my initial offer, if not just plain walk away. Never be afraid to walk away from an iffy deal.

As I approach the meet spot, I like to keep my eyes open for any new information that may impact the upcoming transaction. Here are some first impression red flags that may affect my initial offer:

- Burn-out marks in the road or anywhere nearby
- Broken-down cars or car parts in the yard or surrounding area
- Anything in the area that has been severely neglected (houses, cars, yards, etc.)
- Tools and equipment lying around (This may indicate that the seller has very recently been working on the vehicle.)[23]

Even more importantly than these red flags is the actual condition of the vehicle. It is crucial to be thorough when inspecting a potential investment vehicle. Missing even a small thing could be very costly in the automobile business. For example, I had a friend tell me one time about a vehicle he had bought without completing a thorough inspection. Had he remembered to check the

---

[23] Wrench Tip: I use caution in these situations because I have known sellers to rig up a temporary fix to a major issue right before showing a vehicle to a potential buyer. This deceives the buyer into thinking the vehicle is operating correctly, when the truth is that it has an issue that may prevent it from even making it to its new home.

fluids, he would have seen the milky oil on the oil dipstick. Fifteen hundred dollars and one head-gasket job later, the guy finally had a functioning vehicle. He could have saved a lot of time and money right from the get-go if he had performed a proper inspection.[24]

It is easy to skip over or miss little things here and there, so I created an Inspection Checklist that I use when checking out potential investment vehicles. I've included this Inspection Checklist below so that you can use it as well. This list will help you remember everything that you will want to look over, and will allow you to compile a concise write-up of any issues that you find with the vehicle.

---

[24] Wrench Tip: I had a guy one time try to sell me a 1993 Oldsmobile Alero that looked like it had just rolled off of the show room floor. I mean, this car was CLEAN! Given my initial impression of the condition of the vehicle and the low asking price, I would have been excited to shake hands on the deal, until the seller showed up to our meeting. The seller was a poorly dressed, un-kept, and very grimy individual, who pulled up on a rough looking moped. Something didn't fit here. Because of the condition of the car, I had expected an OCD, neat-freak type to show up, possibly with white gloves and spot-cleaner! Because of the discrepancies between the appearance of the seller and the appearance of the car, I was even more thorough and probing with my inspection and my questions. Not only did I discover an oil leak originating from the heads, but I discovered that the seller was not even the legitimate owner! Be wary of weird circumstances, and don't relax your standards for vehicle inspections, no matter how clean a vehicle may appear!

It is very important to be thorough and vigilant with your inspection. This is decision-making time, and you want to be absolutely sure that you have all of the critical information about the situation and the vehicle before you decide yes or no. Remember that once you purchase a vehicle, it is yours, for better or for worse.

Here is the Inspection Checklist that I use for all of my own inspections:

VEHICLE INSPECTION: AUTOMOBILE OVERVIEW

Year:
Make:
Model:
Color:
Asking Price:
Professional Estimated Value:
Initial Offer Price:
Highest Offer Price:
Notes:

VEHICLE INSPECTION: ADMINISTRATIVE

Seller's Name:
Seller's Contact #:

Title:	Clear	Lien	Salvage
State:			
Taxes:	Current		Not Current
History:	Wrecked		Rebuilt
Notes:			

VEHICLE INSPECTION: EXTERIOR

Paint	Poor	Fair	Good	Excellent
Front End	Poor	Fair	Good	Excellent
Driver's Side	Poor	Fair	Good	Excellent
Passenger's Side	Poor	Fair	Good	Excellent
Rear	Poor	Fair	Good	Excellent
Top	Poor	Fair	Good	Excellent
Glass	Poor	Fair	Good	Excellent
Doors	Poor	Fair	Good	Excellent
Lights	Poor	Fair	Good	Excellent
Tire Tread	Poor	Fair	Good	Excellent
Wheels	Poor	Fair	Good	Excellent
Presentability	Poor	Fair	Good	Excellent
Notes:				

VEHICLE INSPECTION: INTERIOR

Material	Cloth	Leather	Vinyl	Other
Material Condition	Poor	Fair	Good	Excellent
Smell	Bad	Noticeable	No smell	
Seats	Poor	Fair	Good	Excellent
Steering Wheel	Poor	Fair	Good	Excellent
Dashboard	Poor	Fair	Good	Excellent
Carpet	Poor	Fair	Good	Excellent
Floor Boards	Poor	Fair	Good	Excellent
Cargo Area	Poor	Fair	Good	Excellent
Windows	Poor	Fair	Good	Excellent
Gauges	Poor	Fair	Good	Excellent
Shifter	Poor	Fair	Good	Excellent
Radio	Poor	Fair	Good	Excellent
AC	Poor	Fair	Good	Excellent
Heat	Poor	Fair	Good	Excellent
Windshield Wipers	Poor	Fair	Good	Excellent
Interior Lights	Poor	Fair	Good	Excellent
Presentability	Poor	Fair	Good	Excellent

Additional Options/Upgrades:

Notes:

VEHICLE INSPECTION: MECHANICAL				
Start-Up (Cold)				
Start-Up (Warm)				
Rust (Undercarriage)	Extensive	Noticeable	None	
Rust (Under the hood)	Extensive	Noticeable	None	
Battery Age:				
Battery Condition	Poor	Fair	Good	Excellent
Boots	Poor	Fair	Good	Excellent
Steering	Poor	Fair	Good	Excellent
Alignment	Poor	Fair	Good	Excellent
Driveability	Poor	Fair	Good	Excellent
Brakes	Poor	Fair	Good	Excellent
Motor Sound	Poor	Fair	Good	Excellent
Motor Feel	Poor	Fair	Good	Excellent
Shifting	N/A Poor	Fair	Good	Excellent
Exhaust	Poor	Fair	Good	Excellent
Sound:				
Smell:				
Feel:				
Color:				
Particles:				
Fluid Levels				
Oil	Low	Medium	Full	Too Full
Transmission	Low	Medium	Full	Too Full
Brake	Low	Medium	Full	Too Full
Coolant	Low	Medium	Full	Too Full
Fluid Condition				
Oil	Poor	Fair	Good	Excellent
Transmission	Poor	Fair	Good	Excellent
Brake	Poor	Fair	Good	Excellent
Coolant	Poor	Fair	Good	Excellent
Notes:				

Let me take a moment to run through this Inspection Checklist chart with you.

The first section, the "Automobile Overview," should be filled out as you are doing your initial research on a vehicle. Information such as the year, make, model, color, and asking price should be readily available in the advertisement, as well as the seller's name and contact number. As for the "professional estimated value," you will need to do a little research. Compare prices from several sources such as KBB, Edmunds, and Nada Guides in order to get a more complete picture on the value of a vehicle. Using this information, formulate your initial and highest offer prices. If there is anything noteworthy about the vehicle, good or bad, or if you have any questions, take notes in the "Notes" section.

The next section is the "Administrative" section. You can gather this data directly from the seller, or if you would rather use a neutral third party source, the information can also be found in a CARFAX report.[25] A

---

[25] A CARFAX report can be pulled with the vehicle's VIN#. A CARFAX report will give you the registration information, title information (whether the car has been salvaged or junked), odometer readings, lemon history, total loss accident history, frame/structural damage history, accident indicators (such as air bag deployment), service and repair information, vehicle usage (taxi, rental, lease, etc.), and recall information. Current CARFAX pricing is $39.99 for one report, 49.99 for five reports (valid for 60 days), and 54.99 for unlimited reports (valid for 60 days). You can see from the pricing of these packages and the validation limits that if you plan on flipping more than one car

CARFAX report will be able to tell you if the vehicle has been wrecked, how many owners it has had, and much, much more. Use this to determine a vehicle's history and whether or not it has been salvaged.

When you can get your hands on the title, check it to make sure there are no liens on the vehicle (if the seller has the title, there shouldn't be any liens, but weird things happen), and look to see if the title is clear or salvaged. Look at the registration card and the stickers on the license plate to determine if the taxes have been paid up to date. If you have any doubts about the history of a vehicle, make a note in the "Notes" section and be sure to ask the seller for clarification.

The third section is the "Exterior" section. Take note of the condition of the body, the paint, the glass, the tires, etc. Running through the complete list in this section shouldn't take you too long, but it is well worth the time. Exterior issues such as broken windows or bald tires don't necessarily affect how the vehicle runs, but they can affect the resale appeal when it comes time to flipping your investment. Repairs like this are usually very simple to do, but the price of parts can add up quickly, so make sure that you don't get in over your head on cosmetic issues.[26]

---

in 60 days, it will be much more cost effective to upgrade to the second or third package option from the start.

[26] Wrench Tip: A great source of auto parts is the U-Pick or the Pick-A-Part junk yards. You will be able to save a lot of money by finding the diamonds in the rough at junk yards, and you can save even more money by pulling the part yourself.

The fourth section on the Inspection Checklist is the "Interior" section. Note the condition of the upholstery, and be wary of unpleasant smells. Pet smells and cigarette smoke are very difficult to eliminate completely from vehicle interiors, and can be a total deal-breaker for your potential buyers later on down the road. At this point you also need to check the dashboard for functionality. Do the gauges work? Does the radio work? How about the heater and air conditioning? Does the vehicle have any noteworthy upgrades? Make note of anything you see that needs work before you will be able to sell the vehicle.

The fifth, and final, section of the Inspection Checklist is the "Mechanical" section. This is the most important section; after all, the vehicle can look great, but what use is it to anybody if it doesn't provide reliable transportation? Be very careful during this part of your inspection. Unlike the previous sections, where defects are, for the most part, physically apparent, not all mechanical issues will be obvious to spot. Make sure that you get to start the engine cold, meaning that it hasn't been cranked and warmed up yet. Does the vehicle start right away? Watch the exhaust; colored fumes can be a warning sign of something not quite right. Check for rust, check the age of the battery, and check the fluids. You will also need to take the vehicle for a test drive in order to evaluate the brakes, transmission, and steering of the vehicle. Be thorough and ask questions. If the seller is an honest person, he won't mind if you poke around the motor before you make the purchase.

Take a copy of this Inspection Checklist or one that you create yourself with you every time you go to look at a new vehicle (it's also a good idea to keep the checklist after the transaction as part of your business records). Use it to keep yourself on track throughout your inspections. Be sure to look inside, outside, under the hood, under the chassis, and anywhere and everywhere else that you can reach. Listen to the motor when you crank the vehicle up, and keep listening during your test drive.[27] Everything should be smooth and operational. If anything causes you to pause or seems out of the norm, make sure that you can identify the problem, and that it is within your abilities and budget to repair.

Here are some warning signs that could mean a deal breaker:

- Milky oil on the dipstick
- Metal shavings in the oil
- Any kind of smoke coming out of the exhaust
- Strange and unidentifiable noises, squeaks, whines, pops, etc.
- Any burning smells

---

[27] Wrench Tip: Taking the time to do a decent test-drive is important. Listen to how the vehicle runs. Feel how it drives. Preferably, take your test-drive without the seller. This will allow you to focus solely on the vehicle, and will allow you to be more comfortable in testing its limits of drivability. Most sellers will be glad to hold cash or an ID card as collateral in exchange for a solo test-drive.

- Foamy transmission fluid
- Oil in the antifreeze (oil would float to the top, so this would be immediately apparent)
- Dried oil or mud caked all over the exterior of the motor (signs of an extensive oil leak)

While you should always be thorough in your inspections, try to avoid being a tire-kicker. You don't have to be rude or unpleasant to make money in this business. You should keep an easy-going attitude when looking at making a purchase. If you get the deal, great! That means that you were able to meet your vehicle standards and price requirements. If you don't get the deal, or if you choose to walk away, that's fine too. You can always use your capital tomorrow on a different, and perhaps more promising deal. There are always more used cars waiting to be found!

CHAPTER SIX
Sealing the Deal

At this point, you've done your research and you have found a vehicle that you know you can make money on. You have spoken with the owner, and you have gotten a good impression from him. He seems honest and forthcoming with information about the vehicle. The vehicle fits into your vehicle profile system, you have seen the car in person and have completed your Inspection Checklist, and you have communicated to the seller your intentions for the vehicle. Now it is time to make an offer and seal the deal.

Don't be shy about making a lower-than-asking-price offer. About ninety percent of the vehicles I buy, I purchase at a price lower than the seller's original offer. The seller is advertising his vehicle because he wants it to sell. You are making an offer because you would like to make a purchase. Since you and the seller share compatible goals, negotiation should be a relatively smooth process.

Keep in mind the two prices that you should have already written down on your Vehicle Inspection Checklist; the first is the price that you would like to pay, and the second is the price that you are willing to pay. It is time for you to make an offer. Do so with confidence, but without aggression, and look the seller in the eye when you make your offer.

Sometimes it can be intimidating to make that first offer, but the only way to become proficient in negotiation is to just do it. Each time you make an offer, you will become more confident, you will speak more clearly, and you will become more successful. Be honest with yourself, and honest with the people you are negotiating with. Every once in a while you may offend someone, or someone may offend you, but most people are receptive and flexible.

Negotiation is painless as long as you don't take anything personally. Simply inform the seller as to your terms, and he will do one of three things: 1) reject your offer, 2) come back with a counter offer, or 3) accept your offer. Of course, we would all prefer it if our sellers would just take the third option, but that is not always the case. You need to learn to let rejection roll off your shoulders. Business is business, and it's nothing personal. Either you will reach an agreement with the seller, or the two of you will go your separate ways, no hard feelings.

I'll give you an example of a negotiation scenario. Let's say that Mr. Seller wants $1,200.00 for a vehicle, but according to your research and your Vehicle Price Guide, you can only spend between $800.00 and $1,000.00 on the purchase of the vehicle. You decide to offer $800.00.

You say, "Well Mr. Seller, how would you feel about $800.00?" In this instant, it will take less than a second for you to determine how Mr. Seller feels about the prospect of $800.00. You will be able to sense it from the look in his eyes and the subtle changes in his facial expression and body language. In this case, you can tell that Mr. Seller really isn't happy with the lower offer.

He says, "I really need to get more than $800.00." This is Mr. Seller's chance to provide a counter-offer. Most people lack the experience to gracefully present a counter-offer; so now is when you need to step in before Mr. Smith begins to stumble over his words and get defensive about his position.

Remain cool, calm, and collected and professionally ask Mr. Seller, "Okay, Mr. Seller, what do you feel that you need to get for the vehicle?"

Mr. Seller might reply, "Well, I'll need at least $1,100.00." It may be tempting to accept the first counter-offer a seller throws back at you. It will certainly seem more comfortable to accept this offer than it will be to counter with another lower offer of your own. But it is your responsibility to yourself and to your business to pay only what the vehicle is worth to you as an investment, and not what the vehicle is worth to its owner. The money you make as profit will be determined by the dollar amount you spend on the investment. So don't buy a vehicle at retail value and expect to make a profit on it when it comes time for resale.

Here is where you look at the seller and say, "Mr. Seller, I'm sure somebody out there would be happy to pay what you're asking for this vehicle. But for my purposes, I could give you an absolute maximum of $1,000.00 for your vehicle, and I can do that in cash, immediately."

This is when you stop talking. Remember the silence technique from my sample phone interview script? Some people in the business of sales like to say that it is at this point that the first person to talk loses the upper-hand in the deal. Mr. Seller is either going to accept or decline your offer, so don't show any weakness in your position by filling a potentially awkward silence with wasted words. Give the seller a moment to think about your final offer. Often, the thought of cash now will be more motivation than anything else you might say anyways. And remember to walk away from the deal if you can't reach an agreement that works for your business model.

The script above is a generic example of how a typical negotiation goes. Often times, it really will be that simple. Certain situations call for certain techniques, and the more people you talk to and work with the more adaptable you will become in negotiation conversations. I cannot recommend sales training highly enough. There are lots of great sales people that publish lots of great material on sales tactics. If you really want to be great at negotiation and sales, seek out this information at a library, on the web, or from any other sources that you have available.

I want to get your gears turning by sharing with you some examples of negotiation tactics that have worked for me over the years. My hope is that these real life stories from my business experiences will help you feel more comfortable about approaching a seller with a lower offer.[28]

Story Time: 1984 Chevy Corvette

I was browsing Craigslist one morning and saw a fresh advertisement for an 84 Chevy Corvette. The seller's asking price was $2,500.00. I set up a meeting with the owner that same morning that he had posted his ad. I put $2,000.00 in twenty dollar bills in his hands as collateral and went for a test drive. I took my time with the test drive, and naturally I found a few minor issues with the vehicle.

When I got back, I inquired about all the little problems here and there. There was nothing major to report, but when all the little things are pointed at once, it sure seems like a lot to come to terms with. It was no time at all before the seller decided that he was happy to keep

---

[28] Wrench Tip: One method of buying and selling vehicles is to collect as many numbers off of online advertisements as possible and text each one with an offer of half of the asking price. The idea is that, the more people you contact, the higher your chances are of striking a cheap and easy deal. I don't subscribe to this method, but it is one way to do business. In general, I recommend that you refrain from sending someone an offer via text.

the collateral money already in his pocket so long as I was happy with the keys in my hand, and the car as is.

The guy had started out pretty firm on the price tag of $2,500.00; after all, the advertisement had probably only been up for an hour or so when I called.[29] The key here was to take my time with the test drive and give the seller ample time to feel the weight and guarantee of two grand in his pocket.

Story Time: 2001 Cadillac Eldorado

I read an advertisement one morning in which the guy informed potential buyers that he was leaving town in the next couple of days, and needed to sell his 2001 Cadillac Eldorado quickly. The seller didn't have a price listed; instead he requested that interested buyers contact him with any and all offers.

I used information from KBB, Edmunds, and NADA Guides to pull together a decent idea of the price value for the car. I was able to estimate the car to be worth

---

[29] Wrench Tip: The best time to do your online advertisement research is in the early mornings, especially Saturday and Sunday mornings. This will allow you to catch the fresh advertisements and do your research before anyone else can call the seller first. The more interest a seller gets in a vehicle, the more firm the price will become. Use this principle when it comes time for you to sell your vehicles as well. Post your advertisements on Friday night or early Saturday morning to ensure that it will be at the top of the recent posts for the weekend car shoppers.

somewhere between $6,200.00 and $7,200.00 depending on the condition. I knew from the advertisement that there was a decent sized crack in the rear bumper, and that the check engine light was on, although the seller said that the vehicle ran fine.

I called the seller and told him over the phone that I would be willing to give him $4,000.00 cash today for the vehicle assuming that it met a minimum standard that it runs, drives, and everything functions properly. The seller told me that he wasn't sure about that price and wanted to check on a couple of other things. He told me that he would give me a call if he didn't receive any better offers soon. I thanked him for his time and hung up the phone.

I didn't offer a higher price to try and persuade the seller to reconsider my offer. He had shown his cards through the advertisement so I already knew that he was in a hurry to sell, and I was happy to leave him with the option of a guaranteed $4,000.00 cash option, available today. The seller called me back about an hour later and told me that he would like to make a deal.

I took a risk in this situation by guaranteeing the seller a price before I ever saw or inspected the vehicle. But I could tell from my research, that whatever the condition of the vehicle, and it did look to be in great condition, it would be worth investing the $4,000.00. In addition to the cash, I was also offering the guy a quick and easy way out from under the vehicle at a time in his life when he needed financial freedom more than he needed the second car. In this case, the key point to remember is to know both the vehicle and the seller that you are working with, and use that information wisely and ethically.

Story Time: 1997 Isuzu Rodeo

On another of my early mornings of browsing online vehicle advertisements, I found an advertisement for a 1997 Isuzu Rodeo. The seller was asking $900.00 for the vehicle. He disclosed in the advertisement that the battery wasn't holding a charge and the vehicle was idling too low, causing it to cut off at stop lights.

On the phone, the seller told me that he and his wife had just had a new baby, and so they were ready to get the vehicle out of the yard and off of their to-do list. As was the deal with the 84 Chevy Corvette, I made sure that I was the first to respond to a fresh, early morning advertisement.

The seller was hesitant to accept my lower offer of $600.00, but he was willing to hold the cash as collateral while I took the vehicle for a test drive. The weather had been torrential all week, and the sky opened up again as I pulled back into the seller's front yard. The truck drove fine, other than the low-idle issue, and I suspected that the battery issue might be as simple as an incorrectly wired radio. Mud was spattered all over the Rodeo, and the yard was soft enough that the tires were leaving clear ruts in the grass. The whole picture looked pretty dismal.

The seller was still a little doubtful about accepting my offer of $600.00, but it was obvious to both of us that no one else would be looking at his vehicle today or in the next couple days if the rain continued as it was. It wasn't a primary vehicle for his family, and so the seller's major goal was to just get the car off the lawn on out of his wife's line of sight. He decided that the $600.00 was worth making a deal sooner rather than later.

I share these stories with you to demonstrate that if you make a practice out of taking the approach that you can help somebody with an issue, or relieve them of a burden, then you will find your own creative ways to negotiate a great price in a manner that you are comfortable with.

People like to be helped and they like it when other people care about them. People don't like it when they feel taken advantage of or put at risk. So as long as you remember your money principles, what you can pay for a vehicle and what you cannot pay; and as long as you remember your ethics, your integrity, and you treat people like human beings; and you find a way to satisfy the needs of both parties in the deal, then you will have no problems with negotiations.

CHAPTER SEVEN
Now What?

So you've bought an investment vehicle. Now what? If you're anything like me, you probably want to drive home as fast as possible so you can start digging around under the hood. However, there is a very important matter for you to take care of before you ever pick up a wrench; the administrative paperwork.

I know paperwork can be tedious and time consuming, but it is a necessary task for any automobile related business. This should always be done first, because if you do run into any hiccups along the way, you will still have time to iron them out while you are working on your repairs and rehabilitation; this might not be the case if you wait until after the car is fixed to start the paperwork. You do not want the administrative side of your business holding you up when a prospective buyer calls.

The administrative process includes taking care of insurance, taxes, titles, and inspections. Every state has its own rules and regulations regarding these procedures; and so I will keep this chapter brief, and at the end I will guide you in the right direction for finding your state specific guidelines.

No matter which state you live in, the first thing you should always do before you even drive a vehicle home, is call your insurance company and get it insured.[30] I recommend getting full coverage for each of your vehicles; and if your company has a road side assistance program, I highly recommend that service as well. This way you are insured if you get pulled over, and if something happens to the vehicle, the insurance company will typically pay out at book value (which should be more than you paid for it used).

Also, if you for some reason run out of gas, get a flat tire, or break down, which happens more often in vehicles that you are flipping than with your every-day driver, you can use the roadside assistance at no extra cost.

I once had an investment vehicle that broke down on me four times in one month, and I was able to use my roadside assistance to get it towed each time. I have yet to

---

[30] Wrench Tip: Feel free to call around to different insurance providers. Ask each company about the rates it offers and the services it provides. It never hurts to shop around and make sure that you're getting the most bang for your buck when it comes to automobile insurance. I recommend finding a flexible insurance company with quality customer service. I have been able to switch vehicles on and off of my insurance without any representatives giving me a hard time about the frequency of my services required.

reach any sort of maximum limit on tows, and so I have found great value in roadside assistance.

Taxes will be the next step for you in your administrative process as they must be paid before or at the same time as you acquire your new title. Some states allow you to pay property taxes online, but I have found the process to be quicker and more efficient to just head down to the county treasury department in person. This allows me to cut out the week or two of waiting for my receipt to come in the mail. Once you have your proof of tax payment, you can take the receipt over to the Department of Motor Vehicles and get your registration.

Your third step will be to get your new title. You will want to get the vehicle's new title in your name as soon as possible. Sometimes this process can be stretched out to as long as 45 days if there are any issues with the title, or if the DMV is having a busy season. You will want to know about any issues as soon as possible because the titling and the other administrative work is the only thing that you don't have control of once you have possession of your vehicle. You must rely on other people and organizations, such as the DMV, to completely and correctly process your paperwork. I have found that, while most of the time this process goes smoothly, it is always best to give the folks working on processing your title papers a little breathing room when it comes to deadlines.

The final administrative task that you may or may not have to deal with is vehicle inspections. Some states require inspections, others do not. Definitely be sure to look up the regulations regarding vehicle inspections for your state so that you can make sure that everything you do for your business is done correctly by the law. Keep in mind your state's inspection regulations when you are doing your own inspection. If something isn't up to the state's standards, you will have to spend the money to fix that before you can fix anything else.

The main point here is that the administrative side of flipping vehicles is very important, as tedious as it may be. The sooner you get all of the paperwork done, insurance, taxes, titles, and inspections, the sooner you will be able to sell your vehicle. This being the case, it is always best to start this process the day you bring a new vehicle home.

You can look up your state's particular rules and regulations regarding these administrative processes on the privately owned website, www.dmv.org, or by initiating a search for your state's state-operated DMV website on Google or another similar search engine.

CHAPTER EIGHT
Automobile Rehabilitation

Congratulations! You have purchased your first investment vehicle and completed your administrative tasks. Now it is time for the fun part, getting your hands dirty!

The trick to automobile rehabilitation is to get the car ready to sell with as little investment as possible. This does not mean that you should be wrapping duct tape around broken parts and stringing things together with zip-ties. This does mean that you need to fix or replace the things that need to be done and nothing more. It is easy to get carried away with extras, but unless something contributes to the resale value of the vehicle, don't do it! Do not invest in bells and whistles.

Also, you want the car to be as stock as possible when it comes time to sell. For instance, you will most likely not get your money back from investments made towards brand new off-road tires or custom paint jobs. Your job is to get the car in good, reliable working order; let the buyer customize the vehicle however he wants on his own dime.

Your end goal should be reliable functionality (starts, runs, and drives) and the minimum standards of comfort (radio, seat covers, floor mats, etc.). Here are some things that I would consider to be good investments:

- Replacing a broken window
- Replacing a flat tire
- Replacing broken or torn trim
- Replacing worn out floor mats
- Replacing a blown speaker
- Replacing a busted taillight
- Replacing a broken mirror

Start on the inside of the vehicle and clean every inch. Do this before you fix anything. Clean everything. Clean parts of the car that haven't been clean since it was rolled off of the factory line. Clean the trunk area, clean the engine and other parts under the hood, and clean the parts underneath of the vehicle. This can be really tedious and time consuming, but it will make a serious difference between a vehicle well rehabilitated and a vehicle poorly rehabilitated.

When you clean a vehicle, you put your hands on every little part of the car. This process allows you to make a mental inventory, whether you realize it or not, of the vehicle. If something is broken, you will discover it when you clean the part. You will know if all of the buttons are working or not working, you will know where the carpet is worn thin and where it is in good condition, you will know if the paint needs touched up here or there, and so on.

Once a vehicle is clean and you step back to admire your hard work, it will be obvious what the vehicle is missing, if anything. The final touch could be something as simple as floor mats. Or maybe a piece of the trim isn't sitting quite flush and you can fix it with a little bit of adhesive or a new piece of trim. When you are cleaning a car, you are getting to know it on a more intimate level; you will see things and find things that you simply wouldn't ever know about if you skipped the cleaning process.

As for the actual wrench turning, every automobile is going to have a different story to tell, and different needs that must be met. As much as I would love to get down to the nitty-gritty with you, the purpose of this book is not to teach the mechanical aspect of repairing automobiles, rather it is to help people who want to help themselves learn how to build a healthy and successful business around flipping cars.

If you don't have any mechanical experience, don't worry! There are plenty of resources available to help get you on the right track. I suggest that you start by looking through repair manuals such as Chilton and Haynes, and internet sites such as chat rooms and YouTube.

In my opinion, it is best to buy one of the Haynes or Chilton manuals for every vehicle you work on. They cost between twenty and thirty bucks each, and while you can sometimes get away with not using one, they can be a real lifesaver in a pinch. On occasion, I have found myself stuck on a frustrating problem, not even knowing that a simple solution was available in one of the automobile manuals. I have definitely found the up-front expense for the manual to be worth the time and money saved later on down the road.

And if you plan on working on many different types of vehicles, you might also choose to look into the online manual subscription services offered by both Chilton and Haynes. As of the writing of this book, Chilton's subscription plan costs $14.95 for thirty days and $24.95 for one year. Haynes' subscription plan currently costs $29.99 for one year and $39.99 for three years.

As for which manual is better, it is really just a matter of preference. Both companies offer a wealth of valuable information in their manuals, and they are priced very similarly. I personally prefer the Chilton manuals over the Haynes manuals because they seem to have the most relevant organization of easily accessible information about how to do repairs, and how the parts in a particular system work together.

In my experience, the instructions in the Haynes manuals can be pretty circular; meaning that one section will give the first few steps in a process, and then it will direct you to a different section in the book where you pick up your work from there. I suppose the logic here is to save the reader from the repetition of instructions already detailed elsewhere in the book; however, there have been several instances when I have had a hard time finding all of the answers that I needed via the Haynes method.

Over all, Haynes has a workable system. I'm just the kind of guy that doesn't like to flip around a lot when I'm in the middle of a project, so I generally stick with Chilton. It's really up to you which company you go with. Try them both, and figure out which one suits your taste and your methods best.

If you have a problem that you don't quite know how to fix, and your automobile manual doesn't seem to have the information that you are looking for, internet sources such as chat rooms and YouTube videos can have a lot of great "unofficial" fix-it advice. Sources like these can be really helpful, especially in diagnosing and trouble-shooting various issues that may not be detailed, or that you may not know where to find, in a professional manual.

The great thing about these resources is that your teachers are real-life people who have already dealt with the same real-life problem that you are now dealing with. You can learn from their mistakes and also from their successes before you even pick up a wrench.

If the time ever comes when your expertise, your automobile manual, and even your internet resources, can't seem to get you through an issue, I suggest you outsource that particular problem. Find a mechanic, or an electrician, or whatever expert you may happen to need, and call in the reinforcements!

There comes a time in every business when you really have to decide just how much your time is worth. Is your time best spent by beating your head on the hood of a trouble vehicle for three or four days, or is the money you would spend to pay a professional mechanic to get the job done in an hour or two worth saving the days of hassle?

I make the decision to outsource work on a case-by-case basis. I'm not against a good head-beating on those projects that I'm coming up on my maximum investment expenditure limit, but if the expense can be spared with my profit margin still intact, I am never too proud to seek help from the experts.

CHAPTER NINE
The Resale Process

At this point, you should have your administrative work finished, your vehicle should be completely rehabilitated, and you should be ready to make a sale. The resale process involves three steps; the first is to get the vehicle all cleaned up for showing, the second is to successfully market the vehicle through text and imagery, and the third step is to attract and deal with potential buyers.

Cleaning

The first step is to make your vehicle look great. You know that the vehicle is a solid investment, and now you have to prove it to your buyers. You want the vehicle to look like the reliable, every-day driver that it is, and to do this you need to give it that cleaned up, new car treatment.

The vehicle should already be in pretty good shape inside and out from the intensive cleaning that you gave it prior to the rehabilitation process. But vehicle rehab takes time and can be a dirty process, so it's important to go back through everything, inside and out, and shine, polish, and scrub. You will want to make sure to clean both the exterior and the interior.

The exterior of a vehicle will be a potential buyer's first impression. By giving the vehicle a first-class cleaning, you will ensure that this first impression is a positive one. The interior of the vehicle will be the determining factor of comfort for the buyer. The cleaner the interior, the more comfortable the buyer.

In order to make this cleaning process as smooth and painless as possible, I have taken some time here to share with you a few pointers on how to be efficient and effective.

I generally start my cleaning process with the exterior of a vehicle. My three main focuses here are the windows, the body wax, and the tires. Before you do anything, give the car a good scrubbing with some car wash soap. Once the vehicle is free of dust and grime, move on to your windows, wax, and tires.

Make sure to use a good quality glass cleaner on the windows. Quality glass cleaner will ensure that there are no smudges or smears left after you wipe the windows down. Also be sure that you use a tint-friendly window cleaner if the vehicle you are working on has window tint. Some cleaners contain chemicals that will turn tint purple, and unless that is the look that you are going for, I highly recommend avoiding this mistake. I have yet to find a buyer who prefers purple tint over standard! Getting your windows sparkly clean is extremely inexpensive, and it does wonders for making a positive first impression on your buyers.

I also recommend that you wax the vehicle. You can use the wax that you spread on, but I personally prefer spray-on wax. Spray-on wax is quick and easy, and it looks almost as great as spread-on wax. I have also found it easier to avoid smudges and streaks with spray-on wax. Whichever method you choose, a freshly waxed exterior is another way to make a great first impression with your buyers.

Your final exterior job is to freshen up the vehicle's tires and wheels. For this process I generally use a spray on tire-shiner and a good quality wheel polish. You will first want to scrub off any brake dust that has collected on the wheels with your car wash soap. Once you have clean wheels, use the wheel polish to shine off any bits of rust and to give the metal some luster.

The final step to great-looking tires is to spray on the tire shine. This will give your vehicle's tires that fresh-off-the-assembly line look. Once you've used the tire shine, don't drive the vehicle until it is dry. Tire shine is hard to wash off and it looks bad after it has spattered up on car paint. Once you've finished, you can give the tires time to dry as you start cleaning up the interior of the vehicle.[31]

---

[31] Wrench Tip: If there is a license plate holder on the front of the car, either take it off or put a classy plate in the holder so the car doesn't look incomplete. It can be anything, but I recommend staying away from vulgarities, selective humor, and anything political.

Cleaning the interior of a vehicle is pretty simple. First you will want to pull out anything that you've accumulated in the vehicle throughout the time you've spent working on it. Definitely check the trunk and under the seats for any articles of clothing or tools. And of course, make sure you remove any CDs or phone chargers that you might have been using in the vehicle.

Next, you will want to wipe everything down. This includes the door panels, trim, arm rests, dashboard, and anything else that may have collected a bit of dust or a splash of soda or coffee. Be careful about wiping down the steering wheel, some cleaners can make the steering wheel so slick that it can be dangerous to drive.

Once you've got everything wiped down, run a vacuum across the floor mats and the carpets. A house vacuum works fine, but most car wash stations will have a heavy duty vacuum that only costs a few quarters to use. Once all this is said and done, I like to throw in an air freshener to give the vehicle that professionally cleaned smell.

Marketing

At this point, your vehicle should be looking fantastic. You've cleaned up the exterior for a great first impression, and you've cleaned up the interior to ensure that your buyers feel as comfortable as possible when taking the vehicle for a test drive. Now you just need to attract some potential buyers to come and take a look at the product of your hard work. The best way to do this is by taking effective marketing photographs and writing professional text about the vehicle.

Marketing photographs are very important because potential buyers will often base their decision to contact you off of these pictures. When you take your pictures, make sure that you have a nice sunny day. Take photographs of your vehicle somewhere that has a nice background, such as your well-kept home or your freshly-cut lawn. Good marketing photographs will portray a scene that is well taken care of and polished.

Avoid taking pictures that include other vehicles, garbage cans, mailboxes, etc. The car should be the only thing in the photograph, front and center. Make sure the entire vehicle fits in the frame. You want a good, square photo that shows the quality and the work that you have put into the vehicle.[32]

Most advertising mediums (Craigslist.com for example) will allow you to post your advertisement with a few pictures. I prefer to post as many photos as possible in order to give potential buyers a more complete image of the vehicle.

I usually post one photo of each side of the car. I take these shots at ninety degree angles, which allows me to

---

[32] Wrench Tip: Don't take glamour shots of the vehicle with dramatic angles and close-ups of the shine and curves of the body. Leave this for the magazines. Keep your photographs simple, clean, and fresh.

capture the front or back bumper along with one of the sides.

I also post at least one picture of the interior. I have found that the best way to take interior photographs is to sit in the middle of the back seat and aim the camera toward the front of the vehicle. This will display the dashboard, control panel, front seats, center console, and will give viewers a decent idea of what the interior finish is truly like.

The final photograph that I will always include in my advertisements is a shot of the motor under the hood.

I consider these four photographs (side/front bumper, side/rear bumper, interior, and motor) the essentials. If I still have room to post more photographs I will take additional exterior and interior pictures, and also take shots of any of the more positive aspects of the vehicle that I feel will interest potential buyers. These bonus shots could show off tires with great tread, a really nice touch screen radio, etc.

Now that you have your photographs, you need to write your advertisement text. Keep this short, simple, and easy to read. I always make sure to include the year, make, model, mileage, size of motor, type of transmission (automatic or manual), and two wheel drive vs. four wheel drive (for trucks).

After I run through these initial specifics, I will usually highlight the positive features of the vehicle, such as a nice paint job, great tread on the tires, leather seats, fully loaded, etc. The advertisement should answer enough questions so that people can look at the photographs and read the text to get a general idea of the quality of the vehicle. On the flip side, though, your advertisement should not be so detailed that people don't need to call you for more information!

In addition to describing the vehicle, I always leave my first name, email, and phone number in my advertisements. Leaving this information allows people to contact me however they are most comfortable, be it email or phone. I do try to encourage phone calls over text messages by saying something along the lines of, "call Andrew at …"[33]

I have found that text messaging is not an efficient way to communicate with my potential customers. There is no emotion, commitment, or sense of human interaction through text. Texts can be perceived differently than they

---

[33] Wrench Tip: Only leave as much information about yourself on the internet as you are comfortable with. I personally never leave my last name on any internet sites. I also suggest that you establish a separate email account for your inquiries. By leaving an email address for people to reach you at, you are allowing anyone who comes across your advertisement to contact you. I never leave my personal email address. This makes it easier for me to filter through the junk that inevitably comes from posting an email address online. The same goes for phone numbers. There are people who use computers to dial numbers found online. I have found that I can minimize the number of scam texts I might receive by changing numerical digits to letters; for example, I would change a one to an "L" and a zero to an "O." Here is a fake phone number that demonstrates a few different ways to elude computer scammers: (one55) l23-Oll3.

are written to mean, and miscommunication can occur easily. Because of these reasons, I prefer not to communicate with potential buyers through text messages.

I like to let people hear my voice, and I like to hear their voices in return. This allows both parties to develop a mental picture of who they are talking to. People can hear you smile through the phone; it sounds weird, but it's true. You can tell a lot about a person from a simple conversation over the phone. Is he good natured, or high strung? Does he seem sober, or does he seem a little out there? Is he speaking directly and honestly, or is he avoiding questions and giving vague answers? All of this and more can be determined with a simple phone call, and you can be sure that other people will be evaluating you in the same manner.

Don't ask for trust; let the people you work come to their own conclusions that you are trustworthy. Make it easy for them; speak with clarity and integrity, be open about your business and your vehicles, and let them get to know you as a person.

Reaching Buyers

When it comes time for you to start advertising your vehicle, you want to advertise cheaply. You will be approaching the end of your project, and probably the end of your budget. There are several cost effective ways for you to go about advertising.

Do you remember the seller/buyer source pool that we discussed in the section about market research? I've included it below to refresh your memory. Use these sources to advertise your vehicle. Your goal at this point in the game should be to sell the vehicle as quickly as possible, so putting up a few different advertisements in a few different mediums is a great idea.

- Craigslist.com (free!)
- Autotrader.com
- Local Classified Advertisements
- Roadside/Parking Lot Advertisements (free!)
- Networking with Friends and Neighbors (free!)

Most of my buyers contact me through the internet, so I focus most of my advertising efforts into that medium. And if you didn't catch that, I said "buyers contact me." It really is that simple. There is rarely any calling that you as the seller need to initiate; so long as you have done your job with the vehicle, and successfully advertised it to the greatest amount of people, potential buyers will contact you without any more effort on your part.[34]

---

[34] Wrench Tip: Make your schedule flexible, at least when you are just getting started with your business. Answer the phone every time it rings with the intention of setting an appointment. Be proactive and set appointments for the soonest possible time. If you're not hungry for the sale, I guarantee someone else out there is, and that someone is setting up appointments with buyers immediately.

Dealing with Buyers

I believe firmly in the power of words. I hold myself to high standards when dealing with potential buyers. I tell the whole truth about the vehicle, and about what I do with QuickFlip Auto. Conduct your affairs with integrity, and the people you work with will respect you and your business. People like to do business with people they can trust; this is especially true for people purchasing used vehicles. Your buyers will be putting faith in you, and trusting that you are selling them a reliable vehicle. Don't let them down, and both your business and your reputation will continue to grow healthy and strong.

Buyers come in all shapes and sizes, just like sellers do. Some buyers assume that everything is going to be great, and that nobody would take advantage of them. Other buyers will assume the opposite; that everything is suspect, and everyone is out to get them.

The first group of buyers is naturally easy to deal with. These folks are easy going and honest, and they expect everyone else to be the same. The second group of buyers is harder to deal with because they have already made up their mind that they don't trust you. These buyers can be irritable, but don't even worry about it. Just treat everybody fairly and honestly, and most people will respond in kind.

As with every situation in life, you will want to take stock of who you are dealing with and cater towards their personality. Don't schmooze up to anybody, but be likeable. If you see that someone prescribes to a political belief or a religion that you don't follow, don't bring it up and start a conflict.[35] But also don't compromise your character by saying that you prescribe to these beliefs. Just be yourself, and if there are any conflicting points of view between you and a buyer, simply avoid them! You and your buyer have established a business relationship, and the beauty of this is that you only have to talk about business. You don't have to share the same opinions about anything other than a fair price for a quality vehicle. It's that simple!

Make sure that you schedule your business meetings and vehicle showings at a time and place comfortable for both parties. I never meet people or show vehicles after dark, and I always choose a location where both parties will feel safe. This can be your neighborhood or a public place like a grocery store parking lot. You don't want to feel intimidated or pressured, and you certainly don't want your buyer to feel intimidated or pressured either.

The last point that I would like to make about dealing with your buyers is that you should always remain firm on your prices. Remember the difficult seller who knows the worth of his vehicle, prices it competitively, and refuses to budge down any further? That is the kind of seller that you want to be! Because you are not selling your vehicle to someone as a business investment, you don't have to worry

---

[35] Wrench Tip: It is always best to avoid any discussion of politics and religion while you are conducting business.

about your buyers needing room in the price to make a profit.

Know what your vehicle is worth, and make your asking price your rock bottom price. If you go back to my Vehicle Pricing Guide, you will see that I generally price my vehicles hundreds of dollars, if not more, below market value.[36] This ensures a quick sale and eliminates the need for the negotiation process.

If a buyer does try to negotiate, just let him know that you've already priced the vehicle below market value. Explain the work that you have put into the vehicle and why it is such a great value for the price. If the buyer still feels that he needs a lower price, then your vehicle is not the vehicle for him. There will be other buyers, so never be afraid to let one walk out the door. Holding firm to your asking price will show your buyers the value that you place on your services, time, work, and vehicles.

---

[36] Wrench Tip: If I have gotten a really great deal on a vehicle, I usually work in a profit margin of at least $1,000.00 for myself, and then I price the vehicle as low as possible. I like to pass on to my buyers any good deals I may have received on a purchase; so if I can make my profit margin and sell the vehicle for a killer price, I will! Aside from passing on the good will, I know that the best way to keep income flowing is to buy and sell quickly. I would rather sell a car for $2,400.00 and keep it on the market for three days, than sell it for $2,800.00 and have to keep it on the market for a week and a half, because in a week and a half, I could already be halfway through my next project!

So don't waste any time! You're nearing the finish line, and also your payday! Put your advertisement up on Craigslist.com, Autotrader.com, or anywhere else that you can think of. Park your vehicle out by the road or in a busy parking lot with a for-sale sign. Set your asking price as low as you can in order to get people looking at it, and to encourage a quick sale.

The lower your asking price, the bigger your pool of interested buyers will be. The bigger your buyer pool, the more traffic you will get on the car. And the sooner you sell, the sooner you can collect your profit and invest your earnings into a new automobile. Good luck!

CHAPTER TEN
Life Lessons and Experiences

By now, you are an expert on the QuickFlip Auto program. Maybe you've even already started buying and selling vehicles, and maybe you're still reading through this book for the first time. Either way, I wanted to take some time here to share with you a few of my own early experiences with QuickFlip Auto. I am hoping that these stories can shed some light on how the process actually works out in real life. I will share with you a little bit of both my successes and my mistakes, and I hope that you can take my experiences and learn from them just as I have. And so, I would like to introduce to you the Wrangler, the Rodeo, the Cadillac, the Corvette, and the Bronco.

Story Time: 1987 Jeep Wrangler YJ

I bought a 1987 Jeep Wrangler YJ for $2,000.00. This project ended up being a real eye opener for me as to the importance of the lessons I have passed on to you throughout the course of this book. I definitely broke a couple of my own rules on this one.

For one, I went out at night to look at the vehicle and make the purchase, when I knew that I wouldn't be able to see the Jeep clearly and perform a thorough inspection. Two, I drove over an hour away to look at the vehicle, thereby increasing the chances that I would feel the need to make a purchase due to the time invested in the drive. And three, I bought the vehicle based on an emotional decision, as I thought it would be fun for my wife to drive while I was working on it. She had always wanted a Jeep Wrangler, and this seemed like my chance to make it happen for her.

Long story short, I made the purchase and brought the Jeep home. The next morning, I took some time to assess my new project in the daylight. As it turned out, the Jeep was from up north and had way more rust on the body and undercarriage than I had seen the night before. A closer inspection of the motor led me to believe that the original motor had been replaced at some point, thus the mileage of 80,000 was most likely inaccurate. To make matters worse, as I began to dive in to my work, I began to realize that the motor hadn't even been put together correctly.

Within days of bringing the Jeep home, it developed a recurring over-heating issue. I threw several hundred dollars worth of parts into the Jeep, to no avail, before I finally had to take it to a professional mechanic for guidance.

The news was less than stellar. The pros informed me that the Jeep most likely had a cracked or blown head gasket, and that it could require up to a $1,500.00 repair job.

I opted out of the head job and ended up selling the Jeep for only $1,800.00, just to get it out of my garage and off of my plate. I had put about $800.00 worth of parts and mechanics' time into the Jeep, along with an $800.00 set of brand new all-terrain tires.

With the Jeep inoperable, there was no way that I would be able to get my money back out of the tires, so I minimized my loss as best as possible by throwing on a smaller set of used tires and keeping the mud-grips. This also allowed me to price the Jeep very reasonably at $1,800.00, which really helped speed the sale. Even so, I still had a loss of about $1,000.00 on my books.

I tell you this story not to discourage you from the business, but rather to encourage you to stick to your rules and principles. You will be very successful if you keep your head on straight and make wise decisions. The uncomfortable position that I had gotten myself into with the Jeep could have been easily avoided had I stuck my own rules.

Regardless of how deals turn out, I have learned to roll with the punches and never let anything get me down. Just keep working hard and treating people fairly, and you will do good things in your business and your life.

Here are some lessons that I learned throughout my experience with the 1987 Jeep Wrangler YJ:

- Avoid viewing vehicles after dark. You will not be able to conduct a thorough vehicle inspection if you can't properly see the vehicle. In addition to being able to determine the condition of the vehicle best in daylight, it is also much safer to meet new people during daytime and in a public place.

- Always perform a thorough vehicle inspection. Doing so will make sure that you know exactly what you are getting for your money. As I discovered with the Jeep, surprises go both ways, they can be good or bad, and it is always better to avoid the risk of a bad surprise!

- Avoid driving long distances to view vehicle prospects. The longer the drive, the more committed you will become to making a purchase, if only for the fact that you have already invested so much time in the process of going to view the vehicle.

- Avoid making business decisions when your emotions are in play. The second you realize that your emotions are clouding your judgment on a business decision, step away. It is better to walk away from a deal than stick yourself with a dud vehicle because of an emotional decision.

- Invest in functional repairs, not personality upgrades. Although the Jeep looked amazing with those brand new all-terrain mud tires, awesome tires won't make an inoperable vehicle any more enticing to buyers. Focus on allocating the funds in your budget toward creating a reliably functioning vehicle, and you will be successful in making a profit through the QuickFlip Auto program.

Story Time: 1997 Isuzu Rodeo

I bought a 1997 Isuzu Rodeo for $600.00. The vehicle had about 160,000 miles on the dash, and it was four-wheel drive. The mileage was a little higher than I usually like to purchase; but the four-wheel drive worked, which was a huge selling point for my market demographic.

The Rodeo had an issue with the battery draining while the vehicle was parked. The motor would also cut off sometimes when the vehicle was stopped at red lights. The Rodeo also had a replacement fender. The seller had not yet taken the time to paint it green so that it would match the rest of the vehicle. With all things considered, including the mechanical issues, body issues, and the price,

I decided that the vehicle would be a great QuickFlip candidate.

I was actually able to address the cutting-off issue in the seller's driveway before I even bought the vehicle. My vehicle inspection allowed me to notice that the throttle cable had gotten loose. I was able to tighten the cable back up before I took a test drive, and just like that, one issue was already resolved.

When I got home, I took the aftermarket stereo out of the vehicle, as I suspected it to be the cause of the battery drain. In my experience, if a vehicle has both a battery drain and an after-market radio, the radio is usually incorrectly wired, causing the drain. As I suspected, the battery had no issue holding a charge with the stereo removed.

One day as I was driving the Rodeo down the road, another driver cut into my lane and crushed my mismatched black fender and one of my parking lights. The accident didn't cause any other real damage, and I knew the fender and the parking light would both be easy and quick fixes; but the other driver was so unpleasant that I went ahead with filing an insurance claim, figuring that I might as well just let his insurance company pay for the repairs.

The driver's insurance company ended up sending me an insurance check for $1,200.00 dollars to repair the damages. I was able to fix the damages myself for about $30.00 dollars total (I popped the dent out myself, paid

$20.00 for custom spray paint, and found a replacement parking light on the internet for about $10.00).[37]

This is a good example of how easy things can be when you have all of your ducks in a row. I had my administrative paperwork all complete, and when the other guy hit me there was no question of whether I was legally insured or not. I was able to simply call the insurance company and report the incident and that was that. Because I had my insurance all set up, this accident paid for the entire cost of the car and afforded my profit margin. I was later able to sell the vehicle to a family member for only $1,000.00, a price much lower than I would have needed to ask had I not already made my profit margin. And now, years later, the car is still in the family and running strong!

Here are some lessons that I learned while working on the 1997 Isuzu Rodeo:

- If you need a replacement part, check online to see if any sellers are parting out a compatible vehicle, or call around to local salvage yards. These parts are usually in decent condition, and they won't cost nearly as much as if you bought it brand new.

---

[37] Wrench Tip: If you are working on a vehicle with a discolored replacement part, you can custom order the exact color of paint that will match the rest of the vehicle by getting the paint code off of the vehicle information (usually located inside the driver's side door along with the VIN#) and ordering it online.

- Always insure your vehicles immediately after purchasing them!!!

Story Time: 2001 Cadillac Eldorado

I bought a 2001 Cadillac Eldorado for $4,000.00 off of a seller that was in a hurry to make a sale. He made a point to let it be known that he needed the vehicle gone ASAP. The vehicle had only 64,000 original miles, and it was fully loaded. It had an acceptable looking body, with only one defect on the bumper. It also had a great looking interior with black leather, black carpets, and black headliner; it was altogether a very classy vehicle.

I ended up driving the Cadillac for about three months. You know that saying, "drives like a Caddi?" What a smooth ride! I almost didn't want to let it go.

When I finally did put the vehicle up for sale, it got tons of interest and sold quickly. I knew that it was worth between $6,200.00 and $7,200.00 depending on the condition of the vehicle. I had found myself in a position in which I needed to make a quick sale, and so I advertised the Cadillac at my absolute rock bottom price of $6,000.00.

Even this low price should have set me up for a very cushy profit of about $1,750.00 after my administrative work was completed; however, the day after my future buyer called, the cluster in the dash went out. I paid an electrician $65.00 to tell me that, because the Cadillac was a specialized vehicle, I would have to take it directly to the Cadillac dealership to be serviced. This was a week long process in which the car was diagnosed, the part was ordered, and I paid a $700.00 bill. Ouch. I was now looking at a profit of $900.00 and change.

In addition to ensuring that I brought the Cadillac back up to operable standards, I also found myself struggling with a difficult buyer. I typically would never have had both of these issues on my plate, because I don't make a practice of advertising vehicles that still need work. However, the buyer had called me the day before the cluster had gone out, and so he already had the vehicle information and my contact information by the time I had temporarily removed my advertisements for the duration that the Cadillac would be in the shop.

The buyer was a very loud, outspoken person who had no concept of personal space. The guy really wanted the car, he was in a hurry, and he was from out of state. He was actually waiting to make the purchase before he started his trip back home. The buyer insisted on viewing the vehicle immediately, and so, because I needed a quick sale, I took him down to the dealership while the dealership was waiting on the new cluster.

This was a mistake. First off, I broke my policy of never showing a vehicle before it is ready to be sold. Second, I had essentially allowed a belligerent buyer free access to my vehicle by showing him where the car was located, and granting him the knowledge that I would not be able to be with the vehicle every minute the dealership was open for operation.

The buyer started calling me every day with absurd requests and demands, and I later found out that he had been making daily trips to the dealership in order to badger the Cadillac employees for information about the car. He even ordered a vehicle inspection on my tab. The buyer later agreed to pay for the inspection, but I was still not allowed to pick up my keys or my car until he had arrived to pay up. This was seriously inconvenient for me, because at this point I would have really liked to have moved on and found a different buyer.

I agreed to let the buyer test drive the Cadillac after my bill had finally been settled in full. The buyer had more ludicrous demands throughout the test drive, such as stopping at a car wash where he proceeded to spray water up under the hood in an attempt to find something wrong with the motor. After all this, we finally got back to the parking lot and the buyer wanted to negotiate the price.

At this point I was beyond out of patience. I told him, in no uncertain terms, that I would not be lowering the price from $6,000.00. My saving grace in this whole unsavory situation was that I at least stuck to my price. The buyer agreed to the price and then tried to write me a check for the entire $6,000.00, to which I replied there was absolutely no way that I would be accepting payment by personal check.[38]

At this point, the buyer became irritated with me for not accepting his check, which began to raise alarms in my

---

[38] Wrench Tip: It is extremely important to never take checks in any business where you are dealing with people you don't know. There are corrective actions that you can take if a check does bounce, but it is a lengthy and costly process, and it involves court action. It is always best to NEVER accept a personal check for any amount of money that you cannot afford to lose.

head that he was possibly looking to scam me. He told me that he would get the cash tomorrow. He also asked if I would park the car at the hotel he was staying at, leaving him with the keys, and in return he would promise not to drive the vehicle anywhere. More red flags. I, of course, declined his request.

The next day rolled around and the buyer showed up to our meeting with a certified check. Normally I have no problems with accepting certified checks, but because of all of the warning signs I had already seen in the buyer's behavior, I insisted that I needed cash.

We decided to head down to the bank together where I could cash the check before handing over the keys. I asked a friend of mine to wait in the bank parking lot in a separate vehicle, as back up if the situation turned anymore sour. Thankfully, I didn't end up needing his help, but it was close. At one point I was certain that we were going to be kicked out of the bank, and at another point I thought we were seconds away from a physical altercation, all because of the buyer's aggressive behavior.

The cashier started working on the certified check and the buyer insisted that I sign the title right NOW. Trying to diffuse the situation, I filled out the title and left off my signature. Never, ever, sign your signature on a title until you have your cash in hand. Finally the cashier came back with the cash after the check had gone through. I asked the buyer for the title back so that I could sign it. This really set him off as he was under the impression that I had already signed the title. The situation was close to escalating, but he finally took his title and his keys and left.

The point of me telling you this story is that there are some people in this world that are simply difficult to work with. Some people will go out of their way to try and cause a situation and make trouble. Had I not needed the money at that point in my life, I simply would have told the buyer that I would not be doing business with him. As it was, I allowed myself to be placed into a dangerous situation; a lesson that I will never repeat!

Make sure that you follow safe business practices and don't let yourself get into a situation in which you are relying on a particular transaction in order to get the money you need to survive.

Don't compromise your rules and your processes. You want to maintain control at all times when dealing with customers, especially in negotiations and at meetings in which cash and title change hands. Learn from my trying experience with the difficult buyer who bought the Cadillac, and don't repeat my mistakes!

As I look back on this transaction, I am glad that I was able to at least take a few good lessons away from an otherwise bad situation:

- Keep pleasure separate from business. Had I not spent three months driving the Cadillac, I could have sold the vehicle sooner, and to a better buyer, and I would not have had to replace the cluster when it eventually went out. Because it did go out while the car was still my responsibility, I would not have felt right about selling the car without fixing the issue.

- Nothing good ever comes from showing a vehicle before it is ready to be sold. Avoid doing so, and you can avoid messy transactions.

- Don't be too eager to sell, and don't allow yourself to get into a situation in life in which you are relying on a particular transaction for the money you need to survive. Allowing this to happen will place all the control in your buyer's hands, something you don't want to happen. You always want to be able to walk away from a buyer who gives you trouble. Don't sacrifice this control.

- Don't give any more personal information to the buyer than necessary. In my case, I allowed the buyer unfettered access to the Cadillac while it was in the shop. In addition to this, he also harassed the Cadillac service employees to the point where I am not sure I would even be welcome to bring future vehicles in to their service department. And after all of my experiences with the buyer, it is really hard to blame them for feeling this way!

Story Time: 1984 Chevy Corvette

I bought a 1984 Chevy Corvette for $2,000.00. It had about 120,000 miles on it, and it was pretty rough on the exterior. It really needed a paint job, and one of the rotating headlights was stuck in the raised position. The interior left quite a bit to be desired as well; although with a considerable amount of elbow grease, it cleaned up to be presentable in the end.

Fixing the headlight turned out to be as simple as plugging the motor back in. And, as my good fortune would have it, I actually found a guy who paints cars and happened to have some extra paint sitting around that was close to the color I wanted for the Corvette. He was able to give me a $700.00 dollar paint job by using his leftover paint, which was a great price for the work.

In the end, the car was a great little sports car, and I got it for what should have been a good price, but it really didn't fit the utilitarian needs of my market area demographic. It took me about three months to find a buyer. For those three months, I had about $3,000.00 dollars (initial purchase cost, price of paint job, and administrative fees) tied up in the vehicle. I ended up selling it for only $3,500.00. For three months of work, $500.00 really wasn't all that great of a profit.

Another issue that I encountered while I was trying to sell the vehicle is that the 1984 Corvette simply isn't as desirable a year as others. The 1984 Corvette has a design flaw in the fuel delivery system that is well known by Corvette enthusiasts, but that I was not aware of when I made the decision to purchase the vehicle. With this design flaw, the resale value of the 1984 Corvettes just isn't that high. Since it was a specialty vehicle I really should have done some more homework on the details of the car before I made my final purchase decision.

Looking back, the corvette was a LOT of fun to drive, and I definitely got my mileage out of it during the three months it took to make the sale. So even though I only made a $500.00 profit, at least I can cross "drive a corvette" and "own a corvette" off of my bucket list. I don't recommend that you operate your business as I did in these early days, but if a project doesn't turn out quite how you had hoped, it is important to look to the bright side of every situation!

I learned two valuable lessons from my experience with the 1984 Chevy Corvette:

- Do all of your research on a vehicle before you make a final purchase decision. This rule applies especially to any specialty vehicles that you may come across.
- Know your market demographic and the type of vehicles they like to buy.

Story Time: 1983 Ford Bronco

I bought a 1983 Ford Bronco for $1,000.00. This story is another example of how I broke a few of my own rules and went out on a limb for a vehicle. Here were the red flags that I chose to ignore: 1) the Bronco had clearly been worked on by a backyard mechanic, 2) there was a hot wire somewhere in the electrical system, and the electrical system was an absolute mess, 3) the motor was clearly not factory, 4) the mileage was unknown, and 5) the truck was painted in camouflage paint. Okay, I'm just kidding about number five being a red flag. Everyone needs a little camo in their lives every now and then!

You may be wondering why I made such a questionable investment. The reason I felt comfortable enough to do so, is because the price was just so cheap that I knew no matter what happened I would be able to get my money back. For the price of $1,000.00, I was able to pick up a truck that ran great. It had a 460 cubic inch motor that had been cammed, and it was clearly built for power and performance with the transmission geared low. I knew that the thirty-eight inch super-swamper mud tires alone were worth around $1,600.00 brand new. I could also see that the suspension had been lifted twelve to fifteen inches on some seriously heavy duty equipment, also very expensive judging by the manufacturer names hidden under the mud.

In addition to the price being right, I considered the truck to be one of my specialty vehicles. Because I had grown up driving, breaking, and fixing off-road, American-made trucks my whole life, I felt more qualified to determine whether or not the Bronco would be a good investment. After thoroughly inspecting the vehicle, the off-road modifications, and the work that had been done (and would need to be redone) on the electrical system, I determined that I would be able to fix the truck and make a pretty decent profit by selling it to a buyer who knew what he was looking at.

I knew that I would be limiting my pool of buyers with a vehicle like this jacked up 1983 Bronco, and it did end up taking me about 3 weeks to close on a sale. But I also kept in mind when I made the purchase that I live in close proximity to a large military base, and the Bronco was just the type of truck that a single soldier might like to drive.

And so, with all this consideration in mind, I decided to go for it, and I bought the truck. I worked on the electrical issue for a while, trying to get it to hold a charge on the battery (the seller was kind enough to include the portable battery charger in the sale).

Eventually, after spending several days cleaning up the wiring, I decided that my time would be very much worth the money I could pay a professional to fix the electrical issue. I took it to an electric shop where the electricians had done great work for me in the past, and they were able to diagnose and fix the problem for a little less than $300.00; a price well worth the time and money saved, as I would have no doubt continued to pour both into incorrect or inefficient solutions without their assistance.

As for the personality of the vehicle, it was very camouflage-military looking. The entire vehicle, inside and out, had been coated in rhino-liner, and while the outside had been painted in camo, the inside had been left a little neglected (or saved from the abuse, depending on how you feel about camo).

I took the entire interior out of the vehicle and sanded down and repainted the metal surfaces with "flat" black spray paint. I reassembled the interior and moved on to the exterior where I washed down the rhino liner with basic carwash soap, and then I painted over the camouflage with "satin" black spray paint. I used about $100.00 worth of generic spray paint which covered both the interior and the exterior, and it turned out great![39]

In addition to the electrical work, and the personality makeover, I installed a new alternator (about $50.00) and a new battery (about $100.00). The motor ran like a top. The tires were in decent condition. And the truck looked great once it was all blacked-out. My initial investment was $1,000.00, and I put an additional $600.00 and a whole lot of elbow grease into rehabilitating the truck. After it was all said and done, I was able to sell it for $3,200.00, which left me with a nice profit of about $1,600.00. Once I had my advertisements up, the truck attracted a lot of attention. The buyer ended up being a young marine who knew a thing or two about trucks and

---

[39] Wrench Tip: The generic spray paint method worked well for this rough, rhino-lined, off-road vehicle, but keep in mind the type of vehicle you are working with when you come up with your own solutions. For instance, I would probably not have used a $3.00 can of spray paint on the 2001 Cadillac Eldorado!

was more than happy to get the Bronco for the asking price.

The 1983 Ford Bronco definitely ranks as one of my favorite projects to have had the pleasure of working on. I learned a few lessons as I worked through the various issues that came up along the way:

- Don't be afraid to seek the help of experts when you find yourself in over your head on a certain task, as I did with the electrical issues I had with the Bronco. The electricians' services were more than worth the price I paid and the time I ended up saving.

- Advertise your vehicles to as broad a pool of buyers as possible. Even being close to a military installation, I knew that the number of people who would want to drive around a giant camouflage truck would probably be pretty small. By painting the truck black, I opened up the door for a lot of other potential buyers.

- It's okay to have fun and invest in vehicles that you are comfortable with and that you feel you will enjoy working on! Don't feel like you have to avoid investing in a vehicle you think looks like fun. As long as you are certain that you can buy it, fix it, and sell it for the right prices, then go for it! Seize the day!

CHAPTER ELEVEN
Wrapping Up

All right, you now know everything you need to know to start, operate, and be successful with your very own vehicle flipping business. We have covered everything in the QuickFlip Auto program from getting started, getting to know your market, and finding the right vehicle, to learning how to work with buyers and sellers, how to rehabilitate a vehicle, and how to resell it for a profit, and everything in between.

You are now ready to get out there and start doing it for yourself! I have full faith each and every one of you. If I can do it, then you certainly can too. I wish you all the best of luck, and I encourage you to get in touch with me to let me know how you are doing as your business progresses, and also to let me know if you have any questions that I may be able to help you with. And with that, all I have left to say is good luck, and have fun!

Review My Book!

Thanks for reading *QuickFlip Auto: How to Buy and Sell Cars.* If you enjoyed this book and found the information useful, it would mean a lot to me if you would leave a review. It doesn't need to be long, just a sentence or two would be wonderful. After all, we both know that your time is very important as you have cars to flip and money to make!

Contact Me!

I truly hope that this book has given you the guidance and inspiration that will spur you on down the path towards a successful business in the automobile industry. The purpose of all my efforts in writing and publishing this book has been to help people to develop their own healthy and successful QuickFlip Auto business.

This being the case, I would like to invite all of my readers to contact me with any questions, comments, or suggestions regarding either the content of this book or regarding your own experiences. I look forward to hearing from each and every one of you, and I hope that together we can continue to grow and learn as we tackle the everyday challenges of being successful business people.

CONTACT ME AT:

quickflipauto@gmail.com

Made in the USA
Las Vegas, NV
30 October 2020